Praise for *Energy Str*

"Life is energy and when we understand th[
and learn to work with this realm, amazing c[
Ready to release the past for good? Tired of feeling overwhelmed by draining relationships? Then look no further. *Energy Strands* will teach you everything you need to know to become masterful at forming and keeping the life-enhancing connections that matter most."

— **Cheryl Richardson**, #1 *New York Times* bestselling author of
The Art of Extreme Self-Care

"*Energy Strands*, in my opinion, is one of the most in-depth books ever written defining energy and how to use or misuse it. Denise Linn masterly weaves together ageless, divine, and sage wisdom to assist your soul in its enduring journey while on earth. When put into use, the tools she generously shares will assist you in experiencing a life of fulfillment, understanding, and enlightenment. Don't miss out!"

— **James Van Praagh**, #1 *New York Times* best-selling author of
Wisdom from Your Spirit Guides

"*Energy Strands* is a grounded, practical, and much-needed manual for caring for ourselves while navigating the morass of human energetic interaction. A must-read for anyone wanting to live a calm, peaceful, and grounded life in the midst of so much stress in the world. I'll keep my copy by my bedside."

— **Sonia Choquette**, *New York Times* best-selling author of
Your 3 Best Super Powers

"If you have ever chatted with someone and felt your energy drain away, then you know what it means to have an energy cord depletion. Denise Linn knows about energy. She's studied it for a lifetime, and she teaches you how to protect your energy field as well as how to remove negative influences that have glommed onto you from others. This book will one day be known as a classic on the subject of human potential and energy field."

— **Colette Baron-Reid**, best-selling author of *Uncharted*

"Denise Linn's new insightful and educational book, *Energy Strands,* not only teaches you the importance of knowing and understanding how the intricate energy cords that are part of us and the Universe work—but it also teaches you that life is one big continuous circle of giving and receiving energy. You can be in control of this wonderful, intelligent energy and use it to guide you on your path toward happiness, prosperity, and well-being. This book is a must for your library!"

— **John Holland**, psychic medium and author of *Bridging Two Realms*

"*Energy Strands* is probably the most valuable book in the world that we are living in today. It helps us all understand that our connection is far deeper than what we perceive it to be. It proves that we are all interwoven in the subliminal, and yet when we need something or someone needs us, energy never lets us down, it's right there staring at us. That's the beauty of energy! A gorgeous book that's going to be on my list of 'must-reads' for all my students."

— **Lisa Williams**, internationally acclaimed medium and author of *Was That a Sign from Heaven?*

"A master at clearing our energy field and the space around it, Denise Linn isn't just a great author, she's an awesome spiritual teacher. Based upon her decades of spiritual study and profound inner experience, her practical, down-to-earth guidebook to subtle energy, *Energy Strands,* is chock-full of methods for releasing psychic bondage and invoking spiritual protection. Denise shows us how in this must-have book. Read it and use it!"

— **Dr. Susan Shumsky**, award-winning and best-selling author of *Instant Healing* and *The Power of Chakras*

"Denise Linn brilliantly shines her light into the mysterious world of energy and illuminates a transformational process for living life with greater grace and ease. *Energy Strands* not only guides us on how to release aspects of our life that no longer serve us, it also provides the steps to thread deeper connections to people, circumstances, and choices that nourish us. In the process, we are healed. I love this book."

— **davidji**, best-selling author of *Sacred Powers*

"*Energy Strands* is full of eureka moments, laugh-out-loud examples, and the kind of peaceful clarity that I have come to expect from Denise's writings. As usual, she has taken a complex and spiritually important topic and made it crystal clear to the reader. This book has opened my eyes and changed how I see the world, the people around me, and given me a whole new set of spiritual tools that I can use to live a happier, healthier, more magical life—and it will do the same for you!"

— **Radleigh Valentine**, best-selling author of *How to Be Your Own Genie*

"The powerful and easily understandable guidance Denise provides in *Energy Strands* is a life changer! By learning to identify your attachments, and how to release unhealthy ties and foster positive ones, you'll experience a sense of freedom unlike any other! As a highly sensitive empath, I found Denise's book to be both empowering and comforting. I highly recommend it!"

— **Kerri Richardson**, coach and author of *What Your Clutter Is Trying to Tell You*

ENERGY STRANDS

ALSO BY DENISE LINN

Books

Altars

Dream Lover

Feng Shui for the Soul*

Four Acts of Personal Power*

The Hidden Power of Dreams*

If I Can Forgive, So Can You*

Kindling the Native Spirit*

The Mystic Cookbook (with Meadow Linn)*

Past Lives, Present Miracles*

Quest (with Meadow Linn)*

Sacred Space

The Secret Language of Signs

Secrets & Mysteries*

Soul Coaching®*

The Soul Loves the Truth*

Space Clearing

Space Clearing A–Z*

Unlock the Secret Messages of Your Body!*

Oracle Cards

Gateway Oracle Cards*

Kindling the Native Spirit*

Sacred Traveler Oracle Cards

Soul Coaching® Oracle Cards*

Audio Programs

Angels! Angels! Angels!

Cellular Regeneration

*Complete Relaxation**

Dreams

*Journeys into Past Lives**

Life Force

Past Lives and Beyond

Phoenix Rising

*33 Spirit Journeys**

The Way of the Drum

Video

*Instinctive Feng Shui for Creating Sacred Space**

*Available from Hay House

Please visit:

Hay House USA: www.hayhouse.com®
Hay House Australia: www.hayhouse.com.au
Hay House UK: www.hayhouse.co.uk
Hay House India: www.hayhouse.co.in

ENERGY STRANDS

The Ultimate Guide to Clearing the Cords That Are Constricting Your Life

DENISE LINN

HAY HOUSE, INC.
Carlsbad, California • New York City
London • Sydney • New Delhi

Published in the United States by: Hay House, Inc.: www.hayhouse.com® • **Published in Australia by:** Hay House Australia Pty. Ltd.: www.hayhouse.com.au • **Published in the United Kingdom by:** Hay House UK, Ltd.: www.hayhouse.co.uk • **Published in India by:** Hay House Publishers India: www.hayhouse.co.in

Cover design: Charles McStravick • *Interior design:* Riann Bender

Library of Congress Cataloging-in-Publication Data

Linn, Denise, author.
Title: Energy strands : the ultimate guide to clearing the cords that are constricting your life / Denise Linn.
Description: Carlsbad, California : Hay House, Inc., [2018]
Identifiers: LCCN 2017046134 | ISBN 9781401950583 (paperback)
Subjects: LCSH: Energy medicine. | Mind and body therapies. | Mental healing. | Self-care, Health. | BISAC: BODY, MIND & SPIRIT / Healing / Energy (Chi Kung, Reiki, Polarity). | BODY, MIND & SPIRIT / Spirituality / Shamanism. | BODY, MIND & SPIRIT / General.
Classification: LCC RZ421 .L56 2018 | DDC 615.8/528--dc23 LC record available at https://lccn.loc.gov/2017046134

Tradepaper ISBN: 978-1-4019-5058-3

15 14 13 12 11 10 9 8 7 6
1st edition, March 2018

Printed in the United States of America

THIS BOOK IS DEDICATED

TO LUANN CIBIK . . .

MY LIFE IS SO MUCH BRIGHTER

BECAUSE YOU ARE IN IT.

CONTENTS

PREFACE

When we try to pick out anything by itself,
we find it hitched to everything else in the universe.

— JOHN MUIR

Fifty years ago, in front of the Royal Hawaiian Hotel, there
was a huge banyan tree. It may still be there. To a tourist, it was
simply part of an island paradise. However, for those who had the
gift of sight, there was a large shimmering cord of energy that
wove its way out of the tree, through the hotel, and down into the
basement, where there was a massage center. If you didn't know
the center was there, it was difficult to find. Yet every week or so,
someone would walk in and say that they had followed the energy
cord from the tree to the spa.

I worked in that massage center as a masseuse with my
teacher, Morrnah Simeona, who was a Hawaiian kahuna and traditional healer. I was perplexed by this stream of people and said,
"Morrnah, what are they talking about? I don't see any strands of
light emanating from the tree and traveling down here into the
basement."

She gently replied, "When I began to work here, I wanted to
attract like-minded beings, so I anchored an energy strand into
the banyan tree and cast it down to the spa. This is something that
the ancient healers of my tradition knew how to do. People who
were able to see the strand would follow it and make their way into
the spa. Not everyone could consciously see the strand, but they

would arrive saying they didn't know why they came downstairs to my center; it just felt like they were guided or nudged."

And indeed Morrnah did have a thriving business—even heads of state visited her humble massage studio. She continued, "Even if you can't see the cords, strands, and filaments of energy that connect us to everything in the Universe, they're still there. Some empower us and deepen our connection to ourselves and to the Creator; yet there are others that deplete and weaken us. When you understand the nature of these strands, you stand at the center of all that is real and important in life. You know how to stand in the center of grace and personal power." Her words started me on a journey of understanding about the nature of energy and how we are tied to the ends of the Universe.

After those early years with Morrnah, I traveled throughout the world—spending time with shamans and earth-based healers—to learn about the native view of energy and healing. One of the things consistent in every tribal tradition was a collective comprehension about the strands of energy that connect us to the world. Each tradition had methods for strengthening or releasing these strands in order to bring balance into life. In this book, I share some of the methods I've learned over the years to support you in finding greater harmony in your life through understanding these lines of energy.

This book is a journey to help you perceive the cables, ropes, ribbons, strands, threads, cobwebs, and filaments of energy that flow to (and from) you. You'll learn how to use ancient and shamanic techniques to release the cords that bind you and also to empower the strands that strengthen you. It's a hallowed and holy sojourn of the soul.

Discovering and releasing the energy cords that don't empower you is a voyage of letting go . . . and stepping into the flow of life. As you embark on this expedition—and as you recognize and release the cords that restrict you—you may realize that it's time to lay down your burdens. When you become aware of the energy strands that are keeping you from being your authentic self, you discover that there is no one to blame in your life; no one is at fault; there is nothing to fear; and there is nothing about which to feel guilty or ashamed. There is nothing wrong with you. You're okay just as you are. You do not need to hide who you are or put the needs of others always before your own needs. In the moment when you relax and let go, you will know that all is well . . . and it always has been. This is the deeper energy of this book.

INTRODUCTION

The Deeper Truth about Energy Strands

Have you ever chatted with someone and slowly felt your energy drain away, but meanwhile, the person you were talking to became energized and animated? One possibility is that your energy flowed one way, into the other person, and as a result, you were drained . . . and they were revitalized.

Or maybe you've suddenly felt elated, seemingly for no reason. This could mean that someone with whom you have a shared cord of love was thinking of you, and their love traveled on the strand to you. (These kinds of happy thoughts usually energize both the sender and the receiver.) These are examples of how energy strands manifest in your life.

This book will offer you the opportunity to learn what takes your energy up, and what takes your energy down. You'll learn how to release what doesn't serve you in life and how to protect your energy. The soul loves the truth, and the pathway to truth is to be strong in *your own* energy field. You'll discover how to do this from the exercises presented here.

Writing this book created a dilemma for me. On the one hand, part of me doesn't believe in cutting cords and using psychic protection methods, because that contributes to the illusion that we are separate from each other. Yet another part of me—the part that has trained with those in native cultures in energy protection methods—has seen the devastating depletion that can occur from psychic attacks and from people who siphon energy from others.

My challenge was that I wanted to share clearing and protection methods that would work for you in your life, but I also didn't want to contribute to the misconception that we are all isolated from each other. I wanted people to read my book and embrace life with open arms with the knowledge that when you melt the dross off any human heart, you will find pure gold. I was concerned that sharing energy protection techniques might cause you to see the world as a fearful place in which you always need to proceed with care because others can harm you.

Eventually, I decided to step forward and teach you what I have learned over a lifetime of dealing with energy fields. Periodically, I will share gentle reminders of who we are from a spiritual perspective. I do this because it is true—you are not a being separate from the Universe around you. From a divine viewpoint, there is nothing out there from which you need to protect yourself. In the profound sense, it's all you.

This book is for the times when you forget who you are. And as humans, we forget who we are all the time. I do. You do. We all do. That is part of our nature. When we forget, we believe that we are separate from each other and from the Universe. It is in those times of forgetting that it is valuable to understand and learn how to unhook so-called negative strands and expand so-called positive strands.

From a sacred standpoint, there is nothing out there that can truly harm you. I experienced this once, when my doctors thought I was dead after I had been the victim of a near-fatal shooting. The experience was profound . . . and real. I entered a place of golden light that I absolutely knew was my true home. It was familiar. I'd been there before; in fact, it seemed that I had never left. My life on earth seemed like a dream in which the illusion was that we were separate from each other.

In that realm of golden light, which I entered when the doctors were scrambling to revive me, I remembered what I had always known but had forgotten: there is nothing in the Universe that we are not.

The realm that I entered into was so real. This view of reality was very different from the way I had previously experienced life on earth, but it was familiar. My 17 years of life up to that time seemed like a story, and what I experienced in that heavenly realm felt like the authentic truth.

This might not make sense as I recount it to you, but when the doctors thought I had died, I remember leaving my body and being a part of everything. There were no boundaries. I was *one* with all beings and all of life. You were there too. We all were. Everything dwelled inside me, as it did inside you. I knew that we were one.

You are a part of all things. You are the snow-capped mountain in Tibet. You are the breath of a newborn in the Sudan. You are the clean air of the Artic and the smog of Los Angeles. You are the rarified energy of a saint and the angst of a gang member. It's all you. And it's all me. But only in a very heightened state of awareness (or when we're almost dead, in my case) can we touch this truth.

Here in our earthly existence, we believe that people can harm us . . . and they can, because we believe it. We believe that psychic attacks and energy vampires can drain us . . . and they can, because we believe it. It's not just our individual beliefs that account for this. When we trip, fall down the steps, and hurt ourselves, that feels real, and when someone hurtles a negative emotion at us, the pain we feel is real. Simply by being human, we are part of a collective unconscious that believes we are separate from the life around us and that life around us can impair and harm us, and thus it does.

After I came back from the other side, I remembered the truth that we are all one and that we are not separate from the Universe. However, this truth was only a memory. When I slipped back into my body, I was instantly hooked into our space-time continuum. I still took offense at slights. I still felt fear of being harmed. I was still angered when hurt. There were still people who drained my energy. The memory of the truth wasn't enough to diminish the depletion.

I offer this perspective to you in the hope that as you learn how to protect your energy field and discover how to remove negative influences that have glommed onto you from others, you will also hold the awareness that on the deepest levels, it is all you—every strand, every connection, every star and galaxy.

When it seems someone is sucking your energy, it is really the part of you that exists in that other person that is depleting your energy. When it seems someone is replenishing your energy, it is really the part of you that dwells in the other that is replenishing your energy.

As humans, we perceive the cosmic realm as *out there*, as if it were some far-flung location in the stars. We tend to look to the heavens when we think of that place beyond death's door. But the truth is *it's here*. It exists here . . . inside me and inside you. Just as you can tune a radio to different stations—from jazz to rock and roll—each station to the exclusion of the others; the place that we call heaven—the place where we are not separate from each other—is a realm that exists *here now*. It's simply a matter of tuning in to it. You are a spacious being of undulating frequencies, existing everywhere and every place at once. It's just that here on earth you have tuned in to—and we all have—the cosmic station of separation.

Even knowing this, however, it's okay to protect yourself when you feel the need. It's okay to cut cords to others who are depleting you. In fact, it's not just okay to do these things, it's *required* in order to be able to stand in your own light and reach toward higher awareness. However, I suggest that at the same time as you cut cords, you look into your core to find that place within you where the perpetrator lives. Honor that part of you. Cherish it . . . and there will be less likelihood of attracting negative attachments in the future.

You may ask, "How can I love and cherish a part of myself where an abuser or addict dwells? These are some of the cords from others that I want to cut. I can't possibly cherish these things." The extent to which you judge and repress what is called your "shadow self" is the extent to which you will put out the call for these kinds of unwanted things to attach to you. And if you cannot cherish these parts, then—rather than judging them—become the sacred observer. If you can *observe* an unwanted pattern, you can release it; if you *judge* it, it cleaves to you. Whatever you harshly judge, you draw to you. As strange as it might sound, your judgment actually strengthens the cords between you and what you judge.

Jerry attended one of my events; at the break, he came up to me, and in the course of our conversation, he mentioned that all women are bad drivers. He said that almost every day, he was cut off in traffic by a female driver or almost run into by a female driver. It never occurred to him that his strong judgment and belief was actually attracting bad female drivers to him. It was as if a rope of energy unfurled from him, stretched out, and wove its way throughout the city until it found a bad female driver, and then lassoed her and pulled her to him. This is the way judgment strands work. Our need to be right about our judgments can be so strong that we will subconsciously become a magnet for experiences that will validate our beliefs, as Jerry did with female drivers.

The challenge is that it's hard to accept and even embrace things you believe are wrong or bad, but if you can step into observing them—in a nonjudgmental way—it is so much easier to relinquish those negative cords from your energy field. Ultimately, it is a journey of the soul to accept and cherish yourself in all your permutations without hesitation and without reservation, and you'll be discovering how to do this in the pages ahead.

Most of my books are easy to dip into for information in a nonsequential manner. You can cherry-pick a little here and a little there. However, in *Energy Strands*, there is a specific order to the information. In the first chapter, you will learn what energy strands are and which cords of energy are attached to you. You'll learn about the strands that flow between you and friends, family members, acquaintances, and ancestors, as well as those that flow to and from lovers—past and present. You'll also gain understanding about dream strands, ghosts, astral connections, chakras, celestial bodies, and more.

In Chapter 2, you'll discover some of the effects that your strands can have on your emotions and your health, and you'll learn valuable information about energy vampires, psychic attacks, attachments from toxic people, and how residual and predecessor energy can affect your well-being. Additionally, through learning about dowsing and scanning for energy leaks, you'll uncover what strands are influencing you . . . both in your body and in your home.

Then Chapter 3 gives you very specific, highly effective ways to cut and release any cords that are diminishing or weakening you. These are time-honored, powerful methods.

In Chapter 4, you'll learn little-known information about protection—and when to use it. You'll also learn step-by-step methods to seal and protect your energy field, as well as when to use them and when not to.

Finally, in Chapter 5, you'll discover how to revitalize, strengthen, and establish communion, love, and joy cords, as well as how to reinforce your hallowed strands to the Universe. You'll discover a number of ways to create sacred space in your home so it becomes a sanctuary . . . which makes it difficult for anything but vibrant sparkling strands of light to flow to and through you.

You will see that I often repeat similar messages, but in different words. You might even see things in this book that you have seen in one of my other books. This is on purpose. Repetition is the mother of skill. It's also a very traditional way of teaching. So much of my learning has come from native cultures, and the wisdom and stories in those cultures are told again and again in slightly varied ways. It is thought that the best learning occurs in this way.

You have my love and support on the journey ahead. It is a hallowed and holy odyssey of the soul.

CHAPTER ONE

UNDERSTANDING ENERGY STRANDS

*We with our lives are like islands in the sea, or like trees
in the forest. The maple and the pine may whisper to each
other with their leaves. ... But the trees also commingle their
roots in the darkness underground, and the islands also
hang together through the ocean's bottom.*

— WILLIAM JAMES

It is the nature of human beings to get attached to other people and things. (Perhaps this begins when we are born attached to our mother by our umbilical cord.) Our attachments are how we know we are connected to the world around us. The subconscious awareness of these lines of connection is evidenced by our expressions, such as feeling "tied down," or the saying "no strings attached," or "I need to cut the ties." On a deep level, we can sense the strands of energy that attach us to the world around us, even if we can't see them. *They are real.*

1

Energy strands are invisible—yet very genuine—lines of energy and communication that connect us to people, places, and things. Energy can ebb and flow through these links. These strands, cords, filaments, threads, and strings that connect us to the world around us can be thin and transient, or they can flow like a vast river, and they can even come from our past and exist over lifetimes.

Strong emotions, such as love and fear, travel quickly through these linkages; physical pain, physical pleasure, and knowledge and wisdom can also be transmitted through them.

Some of these energy attachments are beneficial; they allow us to feel vibrant and alive. Others aren't so helpful; they deplete and weaken us. When two people interact with each other, energy cords are formed between them. These energy cords can feel either energizing or depleting. Sometimes you can lose energy through a cord. It also can be a way for a person to gain information from you, or even—in a dark way—manipulate and control you. Most individuals are not consciously aware of these energy cords, but they can feel them on a subconscious level. Some clairvoyants and psychics can see these strands of energy, which usually run from solar plexus to solar plexus, but they can attach anywhere on the body. The stronger the emotional connection between two people, the stronger the cord is. Energy cords allow us to *feel* another person, even if they are thousands of miles away. Sometimes we can even sense what another person is feeling or thinking through the cord. Energy strands can pull people together and they can also make it difficult to separate when a relationship is no longer constructive. There are cordlike energy connections to locations as well.

In Western cultures, most people know very little about the strands of energy that connect them to other people and places. They see the world as containing separate and unrelated things. They don't view themselves as a part of all things; rather, they view themselves as something separate and greater than it all. They don't realize that from (and to) every action, every person, and every object flow filament strands that connect to the rest of the world.

Those in earth-based cultures of the past, however, understood the intimate and extraordinary realm of energy. They knew how to sense the strands that improved life and how to diminish and release the strands that did not. In many native cultures, it's believed that humans have filaments of energy rooting us to the land as well as to each other. It's believed that if we travel too far, our cord to the earth will be stretched too thin, and we can become weakened and even ill. The idea of being profoundly connected and corded to the earth is a belief of indigenous people spanning the globe.

In this book, you'll learn what ancient healers have always known: that we live in a universe of energy, and at every point, this energy is influencing and affecting you. You'll learn traditional methods to reclaim your personal energy, cut the strands to toxic relationships and events from your past, and keep your energy field clear. Additionally, you'll discover the connection between energy strands and the collective unconscious, your chakras (the energy centers in the body), guides, angels, the cosmos, and the Creator. You'll discover what the energy filaments connecting you to each object in your home have to do with having clear energy fields. You'll also uncover what strands are supporting your destiny and how to release any that are holding you back.

WHAT ARE ENERGY STRANDS?

I call the cords of energy that connect us to the Universe around us "energy strands"—and also "affinity strands," because the energy of people, places, and objects cannot attach to you unless there is an *affinity*, or in other words, unless there is a frequency match. Here is my definition of "affinity": *A natural attraction to a person, thing, idea, etc.; an inherent likeness or agreement; also it signifies a close resemblance or connection. In the realm of chemistry, affinity is the force by which atoms are held together.* The way I use the term in this book can include a "positive" affinity, which means it can increase your energy, or a "negative" affinity, which will deplete it. These strands can be infinitesimally thin, like microfilaments or spiderwebs, or they can be bigger and stronger, like thick ropes of energy. They can be flexible, flowing, and soft, or they can be rigid and seemingly unmovable. They can be clear, iridescent, and shimmering with light, or they can be dull, sticky, dense, and murky.

Energy strands are not just the etheric and astral cords of connection between people, events, places, and objects; they also serve as a pathway for subconsciously sending and receiving energy and information to and from the people, places, events, and objects around us. Here's how it works between people: When you form a relationship with someone (either in a negative or positive way), malleable energy filaments link you to the other person and them to you, and consequently, information, emotions, and energy frequencies transfer between the two of you.

Highly intuitive people and shamans from native cultures are often able to see or sense these strands. Sometimes the strands emanate from the solar plexus, as I mentioned; other times, they radiate out from other places in the body, such as the third-eye area, the top of the head, the heart-chakra area, and even the root chakra, which is near the base of the spine. The strands can vary in color, texture, and size. Strands formed when two people are in love can be large, radiant, and crystal clear, going from heart chakra to heart chakra. The color can vary from blue to green, and even pink and golden, but the colors are always vivid. However, when someone is resentful of another person, the strands between these individuals can be a murky pea green or a dingy gray, and the cords can be stringy and fibrous.

You can be energized or depleted by what streams between you and another person. In much the way that the ocean ebbs and flows, sometimes you are giving energy and sometimes you are receiving it through your cords, and sometimes you and another person are giving and receiving at the same time.

If you are exhausted and drained after chatting with someone, but they seem vibrant and energized afterward, this could be the result of an energy-strand drain. In other words, energy transitioned from you to that person, but there wasn't any ebbing from them back to you—it was a one-way journey. Hence, you were depleted after your chat.

Energy strands of attachment exist between you and almost everyone with whom you have ever been in a relationship. Sometimes these strands are so thin that they are barely a whisper, and sometimes they are like a Los Angeles freeway. Information, energy, loving feelings, and toxic thoughts can flow back and forth through the strands. For example, you might have the same thought or emotion at the same time as someone that you are cord-connected to, or you might go to the same location at the same time, or purchase the same object, or intuitively know what they are doing or feeling. When the cord is strong, even if that individual is half a planet away, you still may be aware of their emotions, their physical pain, or their thoughts . . . because of the strands that unite you. Sometimes energy strands can grow and become even more solidified, even if you are not in physical contact with the person. You may feel their emotions as your emotions and even feel their thoughts as your thoughts, especially if they are a strong sender and/or you are an open receiver. (It's important to know if the emotions you have are yours, or if they are from someone that you are cord-connected to. In this book, you will learn how to tell what is yours and what is another's.)

Have you ever run into someone you knew when you were both a long distance from where you lived? Of course, this meeting could be a coincidence, but it could also be because of the tug of the cords that draw you together. When you are in close physical proximity, the energy currents between you strengthen and even act like magnets pulling you together. It's almost like a fisherman reeling in a fish; you are drawn together. The more emotions involved in the relationship, the stronger the attraction. (Negative emotions often create a stronger pull than positive ones.) The longer you have known someone, and the closer you are to them, the thicker and stronger the strands are. If you haven't been in touch with someone for years, the strands between you both may lie limp and flaccid; yet when you're in close proximity (or you connect via phone, letter, or Internet), the strands can plump up and strengthen, and even pull you together.

Most people are completely unaware of the effect energy strands have on their life and well-being. In this chapter, you'll learn about energy and discover what filaments, ribbons, strands, and cords are attaching you to the world around you. In subsequent chapters, you'll learn how to sever cords that deplete you and enhance cords that strengthen you.

THREE TENETS (ABOUT ENERGY) THAT APPLY TO ABSOLUTELY EVERYTHING

To gain a deeper understanding of the strands that connect us to the Universe around us, it's valuable to discover some things about the nature of energy in general. There are three tenets that apply to energy cords as well as to absolutely everything. These three tenets underlie everything that you will be exploring regarding the energy that flows out of you and into you.

1. Everything is composed of constantly changing energy.

2. We are not separate from the world around us.

3. Everything has consciousness.

1. Everything Is Composed of Constantly Changing Energy

Those living in ancient earth-based cultures understood that all forms of life—from the clouds to the trees, to the buffalo that roamed the great plains, to mountains and stones—were all transient, swirling patterns of energy. This is an understanding that goes back to primordial times in native clans spanning the world. Our present-day concept that the universe is fixed and staid is dramatically at odds with this fundamental ancestral insight.

We are immersed in an ocean of energy that flows and moves in constant, ever-changing undulations through time and space. All life is energy. Physicists acknowledge that atoms and molecules—even in objects that seem solid—are in constant motion. Beneath the surface of fixed objects—existing in a linear river of time—is a realm of energy that swirls, dissolves, and coalesces once again.

There is an innate harmony and cosmic order apparent in all life, as waves of energy and pulsating electrons spiral into and out of existence. The world around us (and within us) is an interplay of these patterns of energy in an ever-flowing relationship. It is a dance of two opposing yet harmonious forces in the Universe: yin and yang, mystery and form—an infinite yet patterned timeless drama of dark and light.

2. We Are Not Separate from the World around Us

In our dash for technology, we have forgotten the primordial wisdom that all creatures and all things on our planet are connected. We've forgotten that we are connected within a living Universe that sings with life and pulses with intensity of spirit. We've forgotten that everyone and everything has a conscious spirit and that we are all manifestations of pure energy, forever fluctuating.

It's essential to make the journey back to a connected view of reality—that is as innately natural to you as your connection to your mother when you were in the womb—to remember that there is nothing out there that isn't you. Because of the linear way in which we perceive reality, we can't fully understand this on an intellectual level.

Inside each of us is a longing, a yearning, and a remembering of that exquisite place of oneness and unity beyond time and space. We can't communicate about it verbally or even write about it in a comprehensive way. However, deep inside of each of us, we all know this.

Many of the difficulties people experience in the modern world stem from an erroneous belief: the idea that we are separate beings, that we are not intimately connected to our planet and her animals and trees. In Western culture, we believe that we *are* separate from each other, and sometimes we are even divorced from ourselves.

The Western belief that we can exist independently of our environment is an illusion with potentially grave circumstances for health and happiness. It is this belief that makes possible the epidemic of global pollution, hatred, war, greed, and so many other things that fill our newspapers and trouble our sleep. And because of this collective belief about being separate, it's often emotionally difficult to feel our connection to things outside our private domain.

Yet it is essential now that we not only expand our awareness of self to our personal environments, but broaden our sense of self beyond the boundaries of time and space to encompass not just our home, but also our community and our planet.

3. Everything Has Consciousness

Those in native cultures understand what few in Western cultures know. They recognize that not only is the universe around us a vast flowing energy field with which we are intimately connected, *but everything in the universe has consciousness.* Even the most hardened skeptics would agree that animals are conscious beings. And modern science has proven that plants have intent and respond to the energy fields of humans. However, no less conscious are the stones and mountains and rivers. Ancient native people understood this well; they would ask for blessings from the spirit of the sea before embarking on a fishing trip, and give thanks to plants when they were picked, and the animals were thanked after a hunt for the gift of their lives. The earth beneath their feet was not considered inanimate: Earth was Mother. Thanks were given to her, and forgiveness was asked before digging into her flesh, because those in earth-based cultures understood that everything was alive.

From these tenets, it follows naturally that:

1. You are composed of endlessly transforming energy fields.

2. You are not separate from the world around you.

3. The world around you (and within you) is alive and has consciousness.

When you comprehend that there isn't anything out there that isn't you, it is so much easier to understand and release strands that you don't desire.

As a side note, I want to mention that although strands can sometimes be seen as lines of energy, there is a deeper way to perceive them. The reason we perceive them as strands is that it allows us to give definition to something that is essentially indefinable. This is similar to the way that chakras are usually portrayed as colored balls of energy, even though they are more nebulous and not so defined. The colors of the aura and chakras are fluid and constantly shifting and changing, but it makes it easier to perceive them when we think of colored balls of energy. This can also be compared to the way that God is given a physical form in many cultures, because this makes it easier to relate to him/her. It can be difficult to relate to something that is elusive and that is everywhere. So do not be discouraged if you don't "see" the strands and cords that connect you to everything in the universe. The visualization of them is kind of a metaphor to help you understand how and why they work. And when you imagine them as cords, that also makes it easier for all the cord cutting and strand releasing methods to work, and thus for your life to be filled with even more blessings, grace, and love.

In this next section, you will learn about what unique and particular cords and strands are influencing your energy and, as a result, affecting your life. As you read about what you may be attached to, you might want to scan your own life to begin to determine if that precise energy strand is affecting you.

WHAT ARE YOU ATTACHED TO?

Great flotillas of energy strands surge out from each of us into the universe around us. You are not isolated from the world around you; you are tied to all of it. *All of it.*

You have strands to your parents, siblings, children, miscarried babies, childhood friends, sexual partners, difficult or wonderful bosses, and co-workers, plus even sometimes spiritual leaders, therapists, and healers. You may create ribbons or filaments of attachment to public figures, celebrities, politicians, acquaintances, and neighbors. Additionally, there are strands between you and your home and all of its objects, your animal allies, current pets and pets of the past, past lives, ancestors, locales around the world where you have lived, houses you've lived in and where you were born, the stars and the moon, your guides, angels, the Creator, and even ideas and concepts. You do not live in isolation; you are being influenced and influencing the world around you in every moment.

Family Strands

As a baby in the womb, you were attached—via your umbilical cord—to your mother. There was a physical joining, but there was also an energetic connection that lasted far past the time when the umbilical cord was cut. This is why a mother can know her baby is in distress even if she is down the road. The cords are usually strong and it does not matter how far away the mother is from the child, because, in those early years, the cord stretches and distance is irrelevant. Emotional energy surges back and forth between child and parent. Gradually, over the years, the cords diminish and can even dissolve, as the child becomes more independent and self-sustaining.

Sometimes, however, neither the mother nor the child relinquishes the bond, and the relationship can either stay supportive, loving, and close or the parent or the child can suffer if less-than-positive emotions flow between them. For example, you might feel drained when you are with your mother, so you decide to move to another part of the country to gain your independence, but somehow you still feel depleted, especially after contact with your mother. You can have spent 40 years apart, living in different locations, and yet a family member can still drain you. This occurs because the strands have grown thick and sticky, yet they stretch between you both, no matter where you are. Those same mother strands can also be love filled, and the energy flowing through them can gently continue to support you through the ups and downs of life. The same can be true of strands between any family members; however—because of the umbilical connection—the initial strands are often stronger between mother and child.

Strong strands of attachment can be found connecting you with your parents, *even if you didn't know them and even if they have passed over.* Children who were adopted, even if they know nothing about their birth parents, can still have a cord connection with their biological parents as well as with their adoptive parents. Curiously, things such as food preferences, and even religious tendencies, can be transmitted through these strings of energy. The threads between twins are especially strong. Often, though separated by miles, they know what the other is feeling and even thinking. Depending on family dynamics, these kinds of cords can be empowering or diminishing. When the family cords are clear and vibrant, the connecting strands of family members can instill an emotional and energetic support that is sustaining and healing. The reverse is true when the cords are stagnant, dull, and heavy. In other words, *your family is with you no matter where you go.*

Trauma can pass through familial energy cords, and recent scientific research affirms the transmission of trauma through generations. In 2016, the scientific journal *Biological Psychiatry* published an article entitled "Holocaust Exposure Induced Intergenerational Effects on *FKBP5* Methylation," which found that trauma can pass through the genes. Dr. Rachel Yehuda, director of Mount Sinai's Traumatic Stress Studies division, led a study in which her team interviewed and drew blood from 32 sets of survivors of trauma and their children, focusing on a gene called FKBP5. The researchers noticed what is called an "epigenetic change"—not a change in the gene itself, but rather a change in a chemical marker attached to it. For example, in the first generation, the actual survivors of a trauma (such as the Holocaust, the September 11 disaster, or Hurricane Katrina), there's a genetic adaptation or response to that horrendous event. However, in the second generation, which experienced no similar trauma, there is the exact same genetic change. Dr. Yehuda related that when they looked at the survivors' own children, they also had an epigenetic change in the same spot on a stress-related gene. From a spiritual perspective, the trauma that travels through the genes also flows through the family energy cord to subsequent generations.

One of my clients, Laurie, told me that when she was growing up, she always felt irrational nervousness around anyone with a uniform. And when she traveled, she would go into a panic whenever she was asked to show her papers. She said that she couldn't account for these two predominant things in her life until a conversation with her grandmother (her "Oma"), gave her an understanding.

Oma had been a young Jewish child in Nazi Germany, but had never wanted to talk about those times with her children or grandchildren. Oma lived across the country and was estranged from Laurie's father, so growing up, Laurie rarely saw her grandmother and didn't know much about her. However, in one intimate conversation, Laurie's grandmother explained that even though years had passed, she was in continual terror of being taken by the men with uniforms. She shared with Laurie how frightened she had been as a child when she had to show her papers (which were falsified). She was never taken to a concentration camp, but the trauma of those dark times stayed with her through the decades. This is a case where the trauma and fear that her grandmother had experienced filtered through the family energy cords and most likely accounted for Laurie's fears in her life. After Laurie did some cord cutting, her lifelong fear of men in uniforms and concern about showing her papers completely disappeared. You can cut the cord of a pattern, but at the same time keep the affinity cord with a person that you love.

Family strands can have a strong effect on your emotions, even from a distance. However, that influence can become even stronger when you are in close proximity. When someone—perhaps a parent you haven't seen for a while or an old lover—comes into your life, a strand that has been coiled and dried in the corner might suddenly become taut and strengthened. It's like a plant that hasn't been watered and lies limp . . . and suddenly, given water, it becomes upright and alert. Even if you don't see someone for a long time, that doesn't mean there isn't a cord connecting you to them; it might just be lying fallow.

There can also be strong strands to family members who have passed on. Sometimes these are sustaining and supportive, but sometimes they are depleting. If you felt supported and loved by someone while they were alive, chances are that if there is still an attachment after they die, it will continue to be sustaining. If the family member was depleting or needy while alive, however, there is a good chance that if there are remaining strands, they are most likely diminishing ones.

Even if your family isn't your blood family, connecting cords can be strong. David, my husband, and Meadow, my daughter, and I were driving down to the San Francisco Bay Area from our home in Washington State for a wedding. David and I took turns driving. When we crossed the state line into Oregon, we were lost. (This was before GPS.) I was driving, and my idea of navigation is to pull over and ask someone. David fervently believes in *not* asking anyone, but instead relying on a map. This is one area of life in which we disagree. I wanted to stop and find someone who could help with directions, and David grew increasingly angry about that prospect. He was sure that eventually he could figure it out by looking at the map. We rarely fight, but our ire was escalating and we were becoming more and more lost as we meandered through the countryside.

Finally, I declared, "I've had it! The next house I see, I'm pulling in! I'm going to ask for directions!" Right after I made this declaration, we saw a long dirt side road with a small house at the end of it. I careened into the driveway. Dust flew on either side of our car as I skidded to a stop in front of the house. Before David could stop me, I launched myself out of the car and raced up the steps onto a wide porch. I pounded on the front door. I was tired of being lost and I was angry with David for not listening to me regarding directions. It took a while for someone to come to the door, but just as I turned to leave, the door opened.

When I turned around, I saw my stepsister, Sandy. Amazing! I had lost track of her over the years and didn't even know where in the country she was. Yet she was standing before me. Not only did we get directions, but we met her husband and her two girls and we all went out to dinner together. It felt like a kind of miracle, yet because of my understanding of energy strands, I understood how it had happened. It was a perfect instance of how, when two people are in close proximity, long-neglected strands become activated and literally pull them together, like two supermagnets.

Ancestor Strands

In addition to having strands that connect you to immediate family, you also have strands and filaments that travel generations back through the bloodline. In some areas, this is called *ancestor syndrome*. Of course, some similarities with your ancestors, such as eye color and height, can be ascribed simply to genes, but research has found things such as career preferences seem to travel through the generations (even when a child is adopted at birth and knows nothing of their ancestry). What's occurring is that we are each part of a lineage that stretches behind us and unfurls before us. It is an unwavering rope of frequency, light, and energy, through which emotions, experiences, and thoughts (of those who have lived before you) travel to and through you. In many ways, we are each like a young shoot on a very old root. You are connected to your ancestors through ancestral cords.

These strands can be great for you if all your ancestors were noble, gracious, high-minded beings. However, if some of your ancestors were less-than-honorable or experienced massive extended fear, trauma, anger, lack of confidence, or sadness, then these emotions can travel through the ancestral cords and then burrow into you.

In other words, the fear or depression you feel might not be yours personally; it might be an ancestral leakage through the family cord into you.

Sometimes the emotions and feelings that travel through the energy strings from your ancestors can feel like your own because they are so deeply embedded within you. Events in your ancestry that can wobble you are wars, oppression, slavery, famine, and plagues, devastating diseases, crimes, and injustice. Even if you don't know your ancestry, it can still be affecting you because of the cords that connect you to those people and, through them, to those events. However, the great thing is that these ancestral cords can be released; this way, you are not carting around baggage from your ancestry, and also you won't send it forward to future generations.

Kirk, a client of mine, was adopted at birth and wasn't aware of his biological roots until he was an adult. However, he shared that as a very young child, he used to get rocks and "glue" them together with mud to make small houses. His family was amazed at his skill and the beauty of his dollhouse-sized creations. Later in life, when he researched his ancestry, he found that his biological ancestors were stonemasons, and he believed that his skill came from them. In other words, the strands from his ancestors were attached inside him, and their skill flowed through the filaments into him.

Another client, Julie, told me that she always had a feeling of being oppressed and had tremendous fear of authority, especially if the authority figure was of Japanese descent. She was also afraid of speaking up and sharing her opinions with others. She said she didn't feel she was a prejudiced person and she was alarmed by her emotional response around people of Japanese descent. She wanted to find out what the source was.

Of course, there can be many reasons for the way that Julie felt, including current life issues, family upbringing, things that she subconsciously heard as a child, or even past-life issues. However, she did some family research and found that several of her Dutch relatives had been interned in the Dutch East Indies during World War II and had experienced great hardships from Japanese soldiers during that time. She didn't remember her family talk-ing about this with her; however, armed with that knowledge, she then began to understand where her challenges might have come from. (Although these were recent ancestors that could have affected her strands, sometimes we can be affected by ancestor cords from a multitude of generations into our past.)

Julie sent love back in time to her relatives who had suffered so much, and then she cut the cord to those events. Almost instantly, she felt lighter, and later she reported that it felt like a miracle, because her constant fear of speaking up and her fear of people in authority seemed to have dissolved. She shared that she later found herself surrounded by a group of Japanese tourists, a situa-tion that previously would've caused extreme angst (and guilt for feeling that way), but Julie said she felt no anxiety, and in fact was able to easily chat with them.

Friends and Acquaintances

Cathy came to me for a consultation because her emotions had become erratic ever since her best friend started going through a difficult time in her marriage.

"I need help, and I hope that you can ease my situation," she said. "My life is great right now, I'm in a wonderful relationship, I love my job, and I haven't felt this healthy in years, but ever since my best friend started having challenges with her husband, waves of rage or sadness unexpectedly roll over me. It blindsides me every time. After it occurs, I call my friend Sherry and she tells me that at the exact moment I felt the strong emotions, she was in a fight with her husband."

She continued, "My emotions closely match Sherry's feelings at the same moment she's having them. I love my friend and don't want to end my relationship with her, but I need to get off this emotional roller coaster. Can you help?"

It's not uncommon for strands to occur between you and your friends, or even between you and your acquaintances. And if the strands are thick and strong, it's not uncommon to feel your friends' emotions as they feel them. (It's a bit like in the movie *ET*, where Elliott feels everything that ET is feeling just as it is occurring.) I did a cord cutting with Cathy and also shared methods she could use on her own. Later, Cathy happily reported that even if her friend had a fight with her husband, her friend's emotions weren't hammering her, and she was sleeping better. Cathy felt that shifting the strands strengthened her relationship with her friend and brought more balance into her life.

You may even have energy cords traveling between you and casual acquaintances. I find it surprising at times how large and strong these cords can be. John, another client, started to develop a sore throat. He worked as a schoolteacher, so it wasn't uncommon to get colds and the flu from the children, but his sore throat didn't clear up. He went to his health practitioner, but the doctor couldn't find anything wrong. When John came to me, I could sense a gray-green, almost sickly looking strand emerging out of his throat. I asked John if there was anyone he knew who had throat problems, and he couldn't think of anyone. I helped him do a cord release. He was amazed in the days that followed—he said that he'd had the sore throat for almost four months and this was the first time that it didn't hurt since it had begun. (It is not uncommon when a strand is released for associated pain to release with it.) I then showed John how to keep the strands from recurring.

John called the next week with some news. He told me that he found out another teacher in the school (whose classroom shared a wall with John's, but who he didn't really know well) had throat cancer and had constant pain in his throat but hadn't told anyone. John felt that there must have been a strand between him and this other teacher. This kind of attachment is not uncommon. You can have strands between you and another person even if you are just casual acquaintances.

I was at a party once where we were sitting in a kind of large circle in the living room. The owner's cat sauntered in and stretched out, elongated, in the center of the room. She was stretching and rolling in a very sensuous way. I looked at the people on either end of the stretch; there were a man and a woman sitting across the room from each other. They didn't seem to be interested in each other, especially as they were there with other dates. But the cat seemed to be recognizing a strand that flowed between them; she appeared to be enjoying the energy current flowing between these two people. Later, I heard that these two individuals had been having a clandestine affair; even though no one in the room knew, the cat was picking up on it.

Here's another example of how energy strands can work: Dan was a friend of ours when we lived in Seattle. He had been to a number of my seminars and eventually became a helper at our events. He was always supportive of the participants and of my family. I was on my way to the airport to teach at an event in Australia, and he offered to take me to the airport, for which I was grateful. While I was teaching in Sydney, I stayed at a hotel in a beachside town called Manly.

Shortly after I arrived, I went to the Manly pharmacy to get some Band-Aids; as I stood in line, I noticed the straw beach hat of the man standing in line in front of me. I commented about how much I liked his hat, and, as it was a long line, we began to chat.

In a remarkable conversation, it emerged that Roger (the man with the hat) had recently visited Seattle and had met Dan, and in fact, the hat had been Dan's—Dan had given it to Roger! What had occurred was that there were friendship strands between Dan and me, and also some of Dan's energy was still in the hat, so in close proximity, my "Dan strands" began to vibrate; hence, I was subconsciously attracted to the hat, even though I had never seen Dan wear it.

Another way that an attachment can occur is if strong emotions are directed toward you. They can be negative emotions, which can feel like a psychic attack; or they can be positive—for example, if someone sends you overwhelming love. Psychic attacks are real. They can throw you off balance. However, most so-called psychic attacks are not intentional. An individual may become cranky with you and then think about you with an intensity of emotions without realizing that they may be unsettling your energy field. (See Chapter 2 for more information about these kinds of experiences and what you can do about them.)

Before you think, *Aha, I know just the person I would like to wobble a bit by projecting some fiery emotions their way,* remember this: if you use energy in this way—with the intent to damage someone—it almost always boomerangs back to you, and it will create imbalances in your life. Even if you think it might be worth it, it is not.

But please don't feel guilty for anything that may have occurred in the past. If you have been very angry with someone, chances are you didn't create imbalance for them. It's not just the intense emotion that is debilitating to another person. *It's emotion combined with a laser-focused intent that can act in this manner.* Most people have a kind of full-spectrum anger, which means it just radiates out in all directions when they are upset, catching everyone in its field. But it's not a strong field, because it's diluted. It's only when the person has the ability to sharply focus their emotion and their intention on one individual that a cord can throw someone off base.

At the opposite end of the scale, if you love someone and feel the intensity of that love while holding a clear vision of them, this can be healing and energizing. When I feel a wave of relaxation and joy roll through me, I usually follow the cord to find the sender. If it is someone I know, I'll call them and almost always, they'll say, "Wow, I was just thinking of you with lots of love." The great thing about sending love to someone is that there is an instant boomerang effect . . . and more love will flow back to you through the energy strands. The energy flowing on these kinds of cords is healing and beneficial for both the sender and the receiver.

Sometimes, however, if there are a number of less-than-positive people corded to you, you may feel that your chakra centers (the energy centers in your body) are jammed. (It's similar to what happens when so many folks are on their cell phones that it jams the system.) As a result, you may feel constantly drained or overwhelmed, especially if some of the people are needy individuals. (If you want to see which folks have the strongest cording with you, scan your acquaintances; almost always, the first names that arise are the correct ones. See Chapter 2 for information about how to do this.)

So-Called Enemy Strands

Be wary of the cords that come from those you consider enemies or people that do not wish you well. Often the cords are much thicker and stronger between you and those you strongly dislike than between you and those you love. Whatever you focus on—with intensity—strengthens its attachment to you. If you have strong emotions regarding those whom you dislike, that often trumps your love strands, because they are more intense.

I've met many New Age people who will never use the word *hate*, and they say they never think in terms of having "enemies," because it isn't "spiritual." I've known many who say they've never hated anyone or anything in their lives and are appalled by the concept. However, when I look at the cords flowing out of them, some have cords that look exactly the same as those of others who admit to hating or having enemies. In fact, sometimes they are stronger, especially among those who have "religious zeal." Religious zeal isn't confined to traditional religions; there are those in New Age who are just as zealous (and just as judgmental) as those in religious or political groups.

Of course, there are many in New Age communities that have lovely, clear, plump cords of light flowing into and out of them. There are people in all segments of society who have these sparkling strands. These individuals are light, bright beings who truly have never hated and have never felt that anyone is an enemy. They bring vitality and joy to the planet. But there are also many who suppress and deny their anger and resentment toward others and—just like trying to push a beach ball deeper into a swimming pool—the harder they push a negative emotion down, the stronger it becomes.

What you resist persists. If someone resists or denies the truth of their soul, whatever is suppressed becomes stronger, and the corresponding sticky energy that flows through their cords clogs their circuitry. Incidentally, it doesn't mean you are a bad person or not a spiritually advanced person if you feel strong so-called negative emotions. It means you are human. Where the challenge exists is when you judge those emotions and try to suppress them—then they become damaging to you. Suppression actually strengthens the associated strands.

"Enemy" strands, or strands of intense anger, resentment, or bitterness, can seem soldered into your soul. It's natural to want to deny their existence. However, a better strategy is to have a gentle and loving acceptance of yourself, in all your permutations. Step back and observe yourself with compassion. For example, if you notice yourself feeling resentful of someone, rather than judging or suppressing what you are experiencing, say to yourself, with immense kindness, "Oh my, isn't this interesting. It looks like I'm *doing* resentment right now." When you have empathy and acceptance for yourself, cords don't attach in a way that depletes you. And interestingly, they begin to drop away. They no longer have anything to attach to.

Strands from Lovers and Sexual Encounters

There are unique cords of energy that surge between lovers. The intensity of love—and the passion of sexual encounters—creates powerful bonds. These threads can be beautiful, strong, and clear, but they can also be muted, stringy, and dull, especially if there are any issues around sexuality or the relationship. Additionally, if one partner is needy or untrustworthy, then it's not uncommon for the other partner to feel constantly drained because of the strong strands that surge between them . . . *even after they are no longer in the relationship.* These strands are that strong! Even the most casual sexual encounters create durable cords that, if not cleared, can last years or decades. And if someone has numerous lovers and sexual encounters (especially if there is any guilt or shame involved) and they haven't cleared these attachments, the numerous strands can get tangled and intertwined, and can even get in the way of meaningful relationships in the future.

Do you have an old lover whom you haven't seen for a while, but you never truly disconnected from? The strand between you both may have been coiled and dried, yet it can become taut and strengthened when you are in contact, or even if that ex-partner thinks of you. Remember the example of the plant that hasn't been watered and lies limp, but then with water it suddenly becomes upright and alert? This is similar to what can occur with old lovers.

It's important to examine sexual energy strands from your past and clear them; otherwise, the cords may stay for a long time, which can interfere with your current and future relationships. The more intimate we are with another human being, the stronger and more pervasive the cords of energy are and the longer they linger within us. Additionally, even if you are in a loving relationship and plan on being so for a long time, it's valuable to periodically clear the strands between you and your partner, to keep everything harmonic.

It's also possible for someone to attach a sexually generated cord onto you because of their desire. An energy attachment can even arrive from a stranger in public, with a seemingly casual (but intense) yearning focused on you. This is not a good use of their energy and it can disrupt yours. It's valuable to understand this, so you can release such a cord (or shield yourself from it) if it occurs for you. (See Chapter 4 for methods to shield yourself from unwanted energy invasions.)

Here's an example of a cording from a sexual partner: Perhaps an ex-lover feels he is a Master Romeo Superb Lover and believes all of his ex-lovers still want him. When you were together, he might have planted a thick, juicy cord into you with his thoughts. Because it was so strong, even after you broke up, it might still be lodged there, zapping your energy. You might think you have gotten on with life and left him behind, but he might think of you periodically and even replay sexual encounters with you. *Every time he does this, it invests the cord with more energy . . . and it can siphon off a tiny bit of your energy.* Of course, he probably won't consciously know that he is anchoring an energy cord into your auric field, but his thoughts can still be draining your energy.

You might be thinking, *What the heck! That was so long ago and I didn't even like him very much—he was so full of himself. Why do thoughts of him seem to pop out of nowhere?* Perhaps stray thoughts of him are especially surprising because you feel that you have worked through any issues with him and he's just not in your consciousness. Well, it could be that his reminiscences of you are traveling on the cord. If his thoughts are primarily sexual, he might be attaching at the first chakra and even the second chakra. (See Chapter 3 for information about cord attachment and your chakras.) If he is longing for your love, he might have extended cords to the heart chakra. In other words, he's cording you. Again, he probably has no idea that he's zapping your energy.

Of course, he wouldn't be able to connect to any of your chakras with his cords unless maybe there is some "stuff" that hasn't been dealt with—repressed emotions, or unresolved relationship issues, or even family baggage located in your chakras— that makes it possible for him to attach there. In other words, there is a frequency match. Think of a cord like Velcro: *if you don't have a surface for the Velcro to stick to, it simply can't attach.*

Sometimes the cord between you and your ex-lover can be a carrier for lots of spiritual debris picked up from him sleeping with multiple partners and replaying all those moments as well. In other words, anyone he's been intimate with can share the same cord that he has into you, because he might lump everyone together. This kind of cording can cause you to attract negative energy into your life and can make it difficult to attract a healthy and loving relationship.

Strands from Strangers

Have you ever been shopping, or out on the street in crowded conditions, or standing in line with other people, and later found yourself unusually exhausted and drained? Or did you have strange dreams that night? Maybe other times, when you got home after being in a crowd, you felt unclean and that you needed to bathe, even though you hadn't done anything to get dirty. It's not uncommon for energy filaments to hook onto your solar plexus from strangers in crowds or people you pass on the street, even if you are not aware of the individuals. They might not know they are doing it, just as you may not be aware that it has happencd. Sometimes it can feel like someone grabbed you by the arm to speak to you.

The hooks are deeper and a bit harder to dislodge if you are already exhausted. For example, if you are traveling and jet-lagged, and are in a crowded airport where others are tired and out of sorts as well, it's easy to have lots of funky energy attach to you that isn't yours. Unless your energy is strong and vibrant, when you are in a crowd, filaments of energy can glom onto you. However, once you discover these kinds of filaments, they are relatively easy to remove unless emotion was involved, such as someone in a crowd shouting at you or someone flipping you off as they drove by.

If you are with strangers and find yourself crossing your arms in front of your body, this is usually a subconscious way of fending off the attachments from your solar plexus. Often women will hold their purse in front of their solar plexus in a crowd. In addition to keeping their belongings safe, they are also subconsciously protecting themselves from energy attachments from strangers.

Another kind of attachment that occurs in crowds is when, for one reason or another, you have eye contact with someone for a second or two longer than usual, and an unconscious cord reaches out between both of you. And then you see that same person again and again out in public. Maybe you saw her in a restaurant and then saw her in line in a shop and then saw her in a crowd. When this occurs, you know that a temporary cord has attached. This is not bad, it's just something to notice.

One way to tell if you have picked up some attachments while you are out in the world is to watch your dreams for a night or two. You may have dreams that seem unusual. In fact, the energy that is still attached to you will often arise during your dreams. These dreams will feel like "not your dreams."

Pet Strands

Some of the strongest strands are between humans and their animal companions. It's not uncommon for a dog to arise out of a deep sleep and race to the front door in anticipation of his owner's arrival . . . even if the owner is arriving at an unusual hour and is a mile away. What's occurring is that the dog can sense fluctuations in the cord that attaches him to his owner. As the fluctuations through the cord increase, the dog can feel the imminent arrival of his owner. There are many cases in which a pet is lost—perhaps after being taken on vacation with the owners or after a move—and yet travels hundreds of miles to return home. For example, Buck, a three-year-old Labrador, traveled over 500 miles to Myrtle Beach, South Carolina, from Winchester, Virginia, to get back to his owner. Scientists declare that dogs are able to find their way home because of their expanded sense of smell (for cats, it is because they have a sensitively to magnetic fluctuations); however, it's hard to imagine that Buck was able to smell his way through the vast ocean of scents to make it 500 miles home. More likely, he was following the strands connecting him to his owner. (Animals will travel either back to their home or back to their owner, depending on what they are most strongly corded to.)

Emotions also travel in a fluid manner from the owner to the companion. The pet can sense the emotional timbre of their owner and often responds by mimicking the same emotion. Although it's not always the case, it's often easy to tell the emotional state of an owner by observing the emotions of the pet.

Pets can also buffer physical ailments by subconsciously "taking them on" as a way to mitigate the effect on the owner. Often a symptom will appear in a pet before it emerges in the owner. For example, if back pain begins to develop in the owner, it's not uncommon for the pet to have developed back pain first. The back pain frequency travels through the cord between them. Or if a pet begins to develop diabetes, it could be that the owner has a prediabetic condition and their pet is buffering it for them.

Of course, sometimes there is no connection between a human's and an animal's physical conditions, but if it does occur with your pet, there is no reason to feel guilty. Do not demean their gift (taking on your condition) with your guilt. Animal companions take on conditions as a service; they do it with a depth of love for their owner. We each have our spiritual journey, and animals are evolving on their journey just as we are. A pet that mitigates pain and physical imbalances for their owner travels far on their spiritual sojourn.

Although it's unusual, it can also work the other way around: a human takes on a pet's condition and mitigates it or simply reflects it. I was traveling and woke up with a sharp pain in my right hip. I couldn't understand why I had the pain; I had slept in a comfortable bed, I hadn't done anything strenuous, and I hadn't pulled a muscle. I called David, my husband, who was at home, and told him about my pain. He said, "It's strange that you have that pain, because I can't take Sadie on a walk today. It seems that she's also having pain in her right hip." (Sadie is our old, sweet, mixed-breed border collie.) This was a case where I picked up on the pain that our pet was having, and it manifested as pain in my own hip.

Pamela told me that she would often dream about chasing mice and even eating them when her cat, Tam, would sleep on the bed with her. She said she was absolutely sure these weren't her dreams, because in waking life the idea of eating a mouse was repugnant to her, but in her dreams, the mice tasted delicious. She felt she had a strong cord with Tam and that she was tapping into his dreams.

Sometimes the strands are so resolute that the animal's spirit stays close even after death. Maybe you have thought you've seen (out of the corner of your eye) or imagined hearing your deceased pet. Chances are their spirit was close because the strands were still connected.

Occasionally, the strands are so fused that a pet will incarnate into another animal body to reside with the same owner. Carly's cat, Sesame, would only eat her food out of a particular old, dented bowl. Carly thought it was unattractive and replaced it with another bowl, but Sesame plaintively meowed until Carly used the old bowl. No matter how many different bowls Carly tried, Sesame always wanted the same old bowl. So Carly finally gave in and kept it.

After Sesame passed on, a neighbor's cat had kittens. Carly adopted one and named it Cinnamon. As the kitten grew older, Carly began to notice that many of her mannerisms were the same as Sesame's. For example, when Cinnamon was scared, she always raced for the tiny space behind the laundry basket, just like Sesame used to. And she always slept on the same windowsill as Sesame and even snored the same. But when Cinnamon began to loudly meow during every mealtime and sometimes wouldn't eat her food, Carly began to think that Cinnamon *was* Sesame. (When she finally dug out Sesame's old bowl, Cinnamon began to purr and happily ate her meals—as long as they were in the old bowl.)

Carly said, "I have no way of proving it, but in my heart, I know that Cinnamon is Sesame. She came back to me." Some strands survive death.

Strands That Connect Us to Wild Animals

We can also have strands that connect us to wild animals. Many years ago, I spent time with the Aborigines in Australia. The elder of a Northern Territories tribe said that they wanted to teach me some of their ways, but it wasn't allowed unless I was of the same clan. To discover my animal clan, we went out into the bushlands. It was an area sacred to the Aborigines. I was told that the land spirits were so strong there, they would harm anyone who wasn't Aborigine. So, to fool them, I was told to reach down and grab handfuls of the yellow and red ochre soil and rub it all over my body. And then I was given Aborigine sweat to rub over the ochre—this was to protect me so the earth spirits wouldn't harm me. I was then told to sit with my back against a tree and wait to see what animal approached, because the animal that approached would indicate my clan.

I was uncomfortable and hot as I sat on the ground with my back on the gnarled old tree. Ants crawled over my legs. The air felt heavy and oppressive as the dull droning sound of flies filled the background. No animal came. More time passed. No animal came. I was sweating off the "protective" dirt and sweat mixture. I was getting worried about angering the local spirits when they discovered that I wasn't really an Aborigine. Suddenly, a large crow alighted near me. He hopped toward me. He turned his head to the right and then to the left in curiosity as he peered at me. He hopped closer. Instantly, the Aborigines raced forward from their hiding places in the bushes; the startled crow squawked and flew up and away. They said, "We're crow clan too!" The elder explained, "We're the same clan, so we can teach you some of our ways." And that was the beginning of a wonderful connection with the Aborigine culture.

Before this occurred I didn't have a special connection with crows, and I wouldn't have included crows among my favorite birds. However, something remarkable happened. From that point forward, crows tended to gather wherever I was. Once someone remarked, "Do you have a thing with crows? They always seem to gather where you are."

Yes, I did have a "thing" with crows, because during my experience in the Australian bushlands, a strand of energy had unfurled between that particular crow and me, and through that crow, strands of light had attached me to the entire collective crow energy. (When you connect in a spiritual way to a wild animal, often you will find that you are connected to the collective spirit of that species as well.) As a result, wherever I go in the world, it's not unusual for crows to gather in my proximity.

Not only do we have strands connecting us to wild animals, but animals also have strand connections among themselves. For example, migrating birds follow invisible strands of energy that help guide their journeys.

Totem Animal Strands

An animal ally—also called a totem animal or personal spirit animal—is different from a clan animal, as it is the specific animal spirit that is aligned with you. We all have an animal totem (or several). When you are aware of your totem animals, cords of energy connect you to the collective physical animal, as well as to the collective spirit of that animal. This is a powerful and wondrous thing. You can gain energy and activate particular qualities within yourself through your totem strand. For example, if the eagle is your animal ally, it's not uncommon for you to see eagles more often than most people. They will subconsciously sense the strand connection and will be drawn to you. Additionally, strengthening this cord will increase the qualities of the eagle within you—such as independence, being able to see the larger picture, and becoming even more focused and direct in life. To learn how to discover your personal animal totem, see my books *Quest* and *Kindling the Native Spirit.*

Strands of Energy between You and the Earth

In native cultures, there has always been an understanding about the cords of energy that connect us to the land, mountains, valleys, trees, plants, animals, streams, rivers, and seas. Most earth-based cultures believe that when you are born, not only are you connected by the umbilicus to your mother, but there is also a cord connecting you to the greater mother, Mother Earth. The longer a human being resides in their birth location, the deeper and thicker the cord becomes. And the more disruptive it is to one's energy field to leave.

During the time I spent with the Aborigines in Australia, I learned of their belief that there are thick, strong cords connecting humans to the land of their origin. I was told that when one travels, the cords become thin, as I mentioned previously, and this can compromise the health of the human. The longer one lives in an area (especially if one's ancestors lived there as well), the stronger the cords are.

Many times when I invited elders of different tribal backgrounds to visit me in the United States, I was told that the journey would be perilous because the cord might be stretched too thin. They believed that our connection to the earth is similar to the umbilical cord between mother and child. The earth-cord sustains us, just as the umbilical cord sustains the infant in the womb. To be gone too long and/or go too far could be perilous. It took great courage for my friend Nundjan Djiridjarkan, an

Aboriginal Australian leader, to leave Australia and travel to England to reclaim the skull of an Aboriginal warrior named Yagan who was killed in 1833 and whose head was sent to London as an "anthropological curiosity" to be on display. He had great concerns about his cord being stretched so thin but said it was important to reclaim the skull of one of his people.

Not only can there be a cording to the place of your birth, but anytime you move to a new area, your earth-cord reaches out and begins to anchor into the earth. For this reason, when you move to a new location, it's valuable to walk barefoot on the earth. This makes it easier for your earth-cord to sink into the land and anchor you there. Once you are rooted, your body and your energy will be more grounded and balanced.

The idea that cords of energy connect us to Mother Earth may be one of the reasons that those in many native cultures feel contact with the earth is important. There may also be a physical reason for this need to connect with the land beneath us. Throughout history, native peoples almost always spent time barefoot, sitting and sleeping on the earth. Through direct contact (or through sweat-moistened animal skins used as footwear or sleeping mats, which acted as electric conductors) some of the electrons that exist on the surface of the earth transferred into their body. New research suggests that this is an overlooked environmental factor for health, and one that very few living in modern cultures take advantage of. Being in close contact with the earth is called "earthing" and has been found scientifically to have great health benefits. (In Chapter 4, you'll learn about how earthing can help form a protective mantle around you, for protection and safety.)

Mounting evidence suggests that the oscillation of the earth's electrical circuitry helps create a positive environment for the normal functioning of our bodies' systems. In other words, direct contact with the earth allows the electrical flow of the earth to stabilize the bioelectric environment in our organs, tissues, and cells. Moreover, these oscillations may be important for setting the biological clocks regulating diurnal body rhythms, such as cortisol secretion. Research also suggests that direct contact with the earth can reduce acute and chronic inflammation. Emerging studies point to clinically significant positive changes in sleep patterns including sleep apnea and insomnia, pain reduction, reduction in respiratory conditions, better nerve health, and a blood-thinning effect. Additional research shows reduction of primary indicators of osteoporosis, improvement of glucose regulation, and a strengthened immune response.

Our bodies are genetically programed to be in contact with the earth. (It's only been in the last 50 years or so that we have been wearing insulating rubber or plastic soles on our shoes that separate us from the electrical flows of the earth.) Nobel Prize winner Richard Feynman—in his lectures on electromagnetism—states that when the body is earthed, it becomes an extension of the earth's gigantic electrical system, and when this occurs, our bodies move into a natural harmony. Conclusive studies also show that earthing the human body creates significant effects on electrophysiological properties of the brain and musculature. And even a few minutes a day of being in close contact with the earth can make a difference. But alas, most people have only thin cords of connection to the earth. And although there still exists a link intimately connecting our soul to the natural world—the earth, trees, plants, hills, and valleys—this umbilical cord connecting us to the lifeblood of the earth is stretched so thin for most people that it's in danger of severing.

One of the fascinating aspects of cording to the land is in regard to the land of our ancestors. It's not uncommon to experience a feeling of déjà vu when you are in the land of your ancestors, even if you didn't grow up in that area. This is because the dormant cord (within our bodies) to those ancestral lands becomes activated when we are there; it begins to vibrate and plump up.

Russell, one of my clients, knew that his distant ancestors had come from Scotland, but he had never been there until he was 46 years old. He said that as soon as he saw the moors and high mountains, he felt like he had come home. He felt strong, grounded, and at peace. There can be many reasons for this, but one reason is that the subconscious ancestral memories that dwelled within him were activated and traveled through his cords to those lands, and the ancestral memories then traveled back from the land to him.

In addition to the strands that connect us to the earth, seemingly inanimate objects also have strands connecting them to the earth. When I was visiting Uluru (Ayers Rock) and the surrounding area with some Aborigine friends and a friend who worked for the Aboriginal Woman's Council in Alice Springs, I was told to never remove any rocks from Uluru. The rocks were intimately connected and corded to the earth there and didn't like to be moved. (This is conventional wisdom in many native cultures.) It is considered very bad luck to take or move these rocks. A ranger for the area said that he was always getting rocks sent back to him with a hand-drawn map to the exact place that the rock needed to be returned. Evidently, folks had taken rocks and then bad fortune occurred, so they returned the rocks with hopes of regaining their fortune.

Strands from Childhood and Your Past

Not only do your energy strands connect you to places and locations on the planet, but they also are anchored into events from your past. We can have cording to past experiences even back into early childhood, both the traumatic events and the wonderful events. From an energetic point of view, it's best not to have too many cords connecting you to your past. It just clogs your inner circuitry. For example, if as a child you had a frightening experience in which you were bitten by a dog with red fur, a cord attachment might have formed between you and the energy of the event. (Even though something happened in the past, it doesn't mean that it is gone; it can continue to oscillate in your energy field.) This can mean that in the future, if you pass a dog with red fur (or even pass someone on the street who has similar red-colored hair), instantly the cord to that experience from your past with the dog might plump, and the trauma of the original event can subconsciously flow into you. You might get a throbbing headache and not know why. Most of us have hundreds and even thousands of cords connecting us to the past, which can become activated in an instant. These cords can make it extremely difficult to be present in the here and now.

Past-Life Strands

Sometimes location strands can occur between you and places that you have lived before in other incarnations. Have you ever been in a new location and had a strong feeling of déjà vu? Maybe you've traveled to a country for the first time, yet everything felt familiar to you. Not only can strands of energy connect us to the place of our birth and locations in which we (or our ancestors) have resided, but we can also have strands that travel through time, connecting us to other lifetimes. These cords of connection can continue lifetime after lifetime. This is how we find others we've known in other incarnations in seemingly mysterious ways. When there is deep trust and profound love, these cords are luminous and radiant, and they can pull you together again, lifetime after lifetime, like two magnets in close proximity.

When you are in the vicinity of someone you have been close with before in a past life, even if it was a difficult relationship, you become like a tuning fork, and you begin to vibrate or resonate at the same frequency as that individual. Your strands will then pull you together, especially if there is unresolved emotional "stuff," either positive or negative. Sometimes it can feel like déjà vu when you meet them. You can feel like *I know this person*, but you don't know from when or where. Past-life affinity strands can be released or increased in the exact same ways that ordinary strands can.

Contracts, Promises, and Commitment Strands

Whenever you make a commitment, a pledge, or a promise, or sign a contract with the intent to fulfill its requirements, a strand connects you to the energy of that commitment. That to which you pledge has a consciousness, just as people and animals have consciousness. A strand to a concept can be just as impactful as a cord to another person. This is hard to comprehend; nevertheless, it is so.

The bonding effect of commitment strands is understandable when you make a pledge to another person. For example, when you were married, if you said, "I will love and honor you until death do us part," in that moment—when you really meant those words—a strong commitment strand connected you and your beloved. Even if things didn't work out, the cord usually will stay intact, unless it is consciously dissolved. This is why it is often hard to let go of an old relationship, even if you know it's time. The commitment cord still conjoins you.

However, if you pledged with your whole heart to something noncorporeal, such as loyalty to your country, a thread then connects you to the collective energy of your country, which is an idea rather than a thing. And later, if you become disenchanted with your country but haven't severed the cord from your commitment, your energy can be unbalanced because your state of mind is at odds with your commitment and pledge.

Idea Strands

Just as your promises have energy and even have consciousness, so do ideas. This is why it's not uncommon for several people at various places around the world to have the same idea at the same time. The consciousness of the idea emerges and then floats around the ether, looking for someone to connect to. If several people are oscillating at the same frequency as the idea, it will cord to those individuals. To those in native cultures, this is not a strange concept.

When I was with the Aborigines in Australia, I was told that artistic designs and motifs traveled through the invisible realms, looking for someone—usually a child—to adopt and draw them. Sometimes the designs would travel through family lines, so that an ancestor's design would be drawn by a descendant, *even if the descendant had no knowledge of that particular artwork*. Sometimes the specific design would choose someone at random to attach to, but there was always the cultural knowledge that the art had its own consciousness, its own will, and its own desires.

These perceptions from native peoples are reflected in Elizabeth Gilbert's remarkable book *Big Magic: Creative Living beyond Fear*, in which she talks about how ideas have consciousness. She says that although they have no material body, they do have a consciousness and even have a will—they are energetic life-forms. She believes that our planet is inhabited not only by animals, plants, bacteria, and viruses, but also by ideas, which, though separate from us, *can interact with us*! They can come knocking, and if you don't cord with them, they will find another receptacle. Elizabeth states that ideas spend eternity swirling around us, searching for available and willing human partners, and this includes *all* ideas: artistic, scientific, industrial, commercial, ethical, religious, and political.

Strands from the Collective Unconscious

The *collective unconscious* is a term coined by Carl Jung. It refers to the unconscious mind shared by all of humanity. It is a kind of collective reality that we all are connected to and influenced by. Jung wrote that the collective unconscious contains "the psychic life of our ancestors right back to the earliest beginnings." Jung felt that the collective unconscious had a profound influence on human beings. He talked about people having the same kinds of dreams at the same time, and he wrote about the fact that primordial images and archetypes would appear at the same time for various people even though they were separated by distance. Have you ever heard of the same invention, idea, or scientific discovery occurring within days of each other at various places around the world? This happens more than we realize, and it is the result of the effect of our cord connection to the collective unconscious and also to the consciousness of ideas.

There are also various layers of frequencies within the collective, and often we will connect more strongly with one frequency than another. For example, there are strands that connect us to particular cords from religious and political groups, ethnicities, and nations. Sometimes there are hairlike filaments between you and these groups, depending on what you identify with. But sometimes these cords can grow into almost log-sized cords. For example, someone who strongly identifies with being a Catholic will often have large ropes of energy to the collective Catholic energy field. Someone who identifies with being of a particular political party will often have strands of energy to the collective energy field of that party. In the days after an election, many say they feel unusually depressed and depleted (or unusually elated). Part of this is because of the strands of energy that connect them to a collective political energy field. The emotions of many people travel on the strands to their political collective, and these emotions are then amplified and reinforced by the combined energies in the collective field (from many people feeling the same way), which then filters back to anyone corded to that political affiliation. The strands of the emotional collective can even affect someone with a slight affinity to a party, even if they aren't particularly invested in an election. They might feel upset (or elated) without knowing why.

Watching upsetting news can cord you to those events; for some people, it can be almost as if they were there. After the tsunami in Thailand in 2004, many people were devastated beyond measure by it from watching it unfold on television. They were emotional and upset, watching day-by-day film footage of the event. Mary, a woman who knew me from my books, called me because she needed help coping. She couldn't stop watching the news coverage. In fact, she was so distraught about it that she was having trouble breathing between her sobs as she talked to me. Mary also mentioned that she couldn't sleep and was having difficulty functioning because she was so saddened by it all.

Meanwhile, my friend Eric, who was married to a Thai woman and lived in a village a short distance away from the area that was affected by the tsunami, said, "Denise, there is no problem here. Actually, we don't really know anything about it because we don't have television or listen to the radio here." He told me a number of his friends in the States had been calling him and telling him about it, because they were glued to their televisions. He said some were enraged at him because he wasn't distraught about it. Eric said he was surprised by their anger; life in his village was the same as always. The people in his village weren't upset or concerned; it wasn't in their consciousness. Hence, he wasn't depleted by it like so many around the world were. Yet Mary, who was thousands of miles away from the event, was dramatically upset. This occurred because she was watching the horrifying images again and again on television and became cord-connected to the collective event.

I suggested to Mary that she stop watching the news and do something helpful with the time that she would've used to watch television, perhaps volunteering or contributing money to the Red Cross. Mary called back a week later with gratitude for my suggestion about the Red Cross. She said as soon as she started taking action (and stopped watching the news), she felt better.

After the presidential inauguration in the United States in 2017, many people contacted me, sharing their extreme angst. Some said they were so distressed that they had physical symptoms, such as headaches, upset stomachs, and constricted breathing. Many shared their rage and depression and talked about how their emotions were creating havoc in their lives. Some were calling because they were angry with the people that were upset. They said, "They should get over it!" In every case, each of these people had been glued to some kind of media throughout the election, either television or the Internet. They were feeding their angst into the collective cloud of churning emotions, and the collective of all those negative feelings was cycling back to them with more vigor.

My husband and I don't have television reception, and consequently, we don't watch the immediate visual horror of wars, hurricanes, tsunamis, earthquakes, political dissent, and so on. We do stay in touch with world events—through listening to the radio or reading newspapers—but we don't watch the riveting events unfolding moment by moment on mass media. We've found that it's almost impossible to not cord-connect to the collective unconscious of world events when watching the visual coverage.

It's good to know what's occurring in your world, but when you become distraught over an event that you can't change and can't help, it depletes you, and it diminishes your ability to make a positive impact in the world. If you do feel compelled to watch visual news of the disasters of the world, here is a suggestion: Don't just stew in your emotions; do something. Go on a march,

volunteer your time, make a donation, call or write your represen-
tatives, or make phone calls to other organizations. Take action on
the things you care about. Don't allow your energy frequency to
lower to the point where you become ill or emotionally disabled.

Dream Strands

I was awakened in the morning, caressed by remnants of a
lovely dream . . . about seaweed. To my recollection, I had never
dreamed of seaweed before, nor was seaweed something I usually thought about. It just wasn't on my radar. So it was a curious dream. Later that day, I decided to call my sister, Heather. We
hadn't been in touch for a number of months. In the course of
our call, she said that she had fallen asleep reading a book about
seaweed. I then understood my dream.

What had occurred was that her thoughts about seaweed—
that she had just before she fell asleep—had traveled on the cord
that connected us. These images of seaweed traveling on the
strand plumped it up, which resulted in me having the idea to call
Heather. It's not unusual for the thoughts and emotions of those
with whom we are corded to show up in our dreams.

There are not usually strands connected to your actual noc-
turnal dreams, but the things you are corded to will often appear
in your nighttime dramas. Your dreams can begin to give you a
clearer idea of where your energy attachments are . . . and which
ones you should increase or release.

As you chronicle and journal about your dreams, you can
begin to discover what you are corded to. Pay particular attention
to repetitive dreams and to nightmares. There are often clues in
both these kinds of dreams.

Here's an example of how you can discover affinity strands in
your dreams: Laura, one of my students, had a disturbing dream
in which she was in a bakery where most of the baked goods were
hot cross buns. These are sweet rolls with a sugary cross of icing
on top. As a child, Laura used to sing the nursery rhyme about hot
cross buns. In her dream, when she tried to pick a bun up, it was

hot, and she felt like her hand was being yanked into the bun. She couldn't pull it out, and she felt frightened.

When Laura examined the dream, she thought about her new boss's last name, which happened to be Cross. When he had met her on his first day, under his breath he had said, "Well, you're hot!" He was paying special attention to her at work, which was very unsettling. She said she needed the job and didn't want to make waves at the office, but she sensed that he had hooked an energy strand into her, and it was exhausting her.

Laura used some of the methods that you will learn later in this book, and said, "Denise, it's almost like a miracle occurred after I used your releasing methods. I used to feel Mr. Cross watching me at work. Sometimes it even felt like he was undressing me with his eyes. I hated going to work because of him. But I used your cord-cutting method one evening, and when I went into work the next day, it was like he didn't see me. It was wonderful. Since that time, I have been able to be at work with comfort. Amazingly, he was fired not long after that—I don't know why—but now we have a boss that we all love. Isn't it great how things worked out?"

Your dreams can indicate cord attachments that you may not even be aware of, but that nevertheless are draining your energy, so it's valuable to remember and examine them. As with any dreamwork, you might consider investing in a journal to write down your dreams immediately upon waking. (Most dreams are forgotten within ten minutes of waking, so it is essential to write them down.)

Astral Attachment Strands

Have you ever walked through a bar or a casino and felt unclean or depleted afterward, or later noticed that your emotions were on a roller coaster? It could be that an "astral being" attached to you while you were in the bar. Not all astral attachments will take your energy down, but many of them will. Astral attachments, also called entity attachments, can come in many forms.

Just as in the physical realm, where harmful bacteria, viruses, and parasites wreak havoc in our lives, there are also nonphysical kinds of pathogens that can attach to us and disrupt our lives. They are etheric beings that are generated by human thoughts that have been infused with emotion and intent. Astral entities more or less float around in the ether and can latch on to someone who is vulnerable, overly open, or tired. They can feel and even look parasitic. Clairvoyants describe them as appearing in various grotesque forms. The first time I "saw" these entities, I was in the hospital after my dramatic near-death trauma when I was seventeen. There were quite a lot of these misshapen "beings" in the hospital hallways and in the hospital rooms. Some floated around, others were glued to a hospital bed or chair . . . and they seemed to influence the thoughts and emotions of those near them. Many of them looked like gremlins or trolls. They looked so real that I was surprised no one else seemed to see them. The great news is that entity attachments are fairly easy to remove. (See Chapter 3 for methods to remove astral attachments.)

Some of the most damaging astral attachments are glued onto folks who have taken a lot of drugs or who are habitually drunk. Drugs, such as methamphetamines, seem to create the largest rips in one's auric field and it's not uncommon to see quite a number of astral attachments on a meth addict, to the point where sometimes these beings cloud or even overtake the person's personality.

When our home was being built, one of the builders had a number of laborers who worked for him. One laborer, who I will call Raymond, was a happy-go-lucky guy. He was a joy to be around and he always looked for what was positive in the world. When our beloved dog, Pepper, died, Raymond kindly dug the grave for him, for which we'll always be grateful. One day I was chatting with Raymond, and suddenly—seemingly out of nowhere—his eyes turned black and his face seemed to contort into a hideous, dark demon. It was like a completely different person was peering into me. I was frightened and shocked. It felt like something out of a horror movie.

Then, just as suddenly, his face dissolved back to his normal features, and I was talking to Raymond again. He didn't seem to be aware that anything had happened . . . and he just kept chatting.

When I "scanned" him later, however, I saw that he had numerous astral attachments bored into him. The next day, he didn't turn up for work, and we later heard that he had been taking meth, had committed some robberies, and was put in jail. Eventually, when he got out of jail, his mannerisms and words were so erratic that his family members placed him in a mental institution.

It's not uncommon for astral entity attachments to become so numerous that they overcome a person's natural personality. Raymond is a wonderful human being, but the holes left in his auric field—from taking meth—allowed dark entities to attach to him. Their energy together was stronger than his innate personality . . . and they eventually took over. (It is possible that a drug addict can have a strong, vibrant, sparkling energy field, with no attachments, but it takes a focused, disciplined personality, and this is highly unusual.)

Do not be concerned about astral entities taking over you or making you mentally ill. *They can't knock you for a loop unless you are about to get knocked over anyway.* They can only attach to something within you that is a frequency match. Many people very mistakenly attribute some of the negative things in their lives to entities and astral beings, which in actuality is a way of not owning the challenges in their lives. In other words, they haven't taken responsibility for the difficulties in their lives, so they erroneously place the blame on astral beings. If someone constantly believes that entities and astral beings are mucking up their life, chances are they are giving them way too much power, or they are a chronic victim of life, or subconsciously they enjoy the added drama in their life. (See Chapter 3 to clear astral entity attachments from your energy field.)

Ghosts and Earthbound Spirit Attachments

Astral attachments are different from ghosts. A ghost is an earthbound soul, or discarnate being, who died but hasn't managed to get to the other side. It is stuck on the earth plane, usually because of a strong connection to a place, event, or person. It can be incredibly draining to have a ghost strand attach to you. Everything feels harder to accomplish. It can feel like there is a weight on your shoulders and a constriction in your chest. Luckily, it's very rare to have a ghost attachment—but it can happen, most usually if the ghost was someone you knew when they were alive or if they are strongly attached to your place of residence.

As with every other kind of cord attachment, a ghost can only wobble you if there is some kind of frequency match. Someone can live in a house for 20 years with a ghost and never know it and never be bothered by it if there is no frequency match and if there is nothing for the ghost to hook into. Then a visitor can be in the house overnight and have ghostly experiences. In other words, an energy strand forms between the ghost and the visitor, but only if something within the visitor matches something within the ghost. For example, if the ghost was a closet alcoholic when she was alive, and the visitor is also a closet alcoholic, this might form a strand between the two of them.

It's important to remember that ghosts cannot hurt you; it is your fear that hurts you. Although they can make you feel afraid, it is the fear that creates challenges, and not the ghost. When Sam, a man who attends my seminars, encountered a ghost, he tried to run and banged into the wall. He assumed the ghost pushed him into the wall. But when he replayed the events, he realized that he was so afraid that he ran into the wall—the ghost didn't push him. *Your fear* can even create phenomena such as doors slamming, feelings of being pushed, or things floating. The psychic energy of fear can affect physical objects. Additionally, fear actually makes the ghost cling more tightly to you, so it's important to step into your courage. You have a body; they don't. *You* are in control. Let go of fear and step into grace, sympathy, and love, and the ghost cords will dissolve.

The best way to clear ghosts is to treat them like dear friends going through a hard time. Gently, graciously, and lovingly say something like, "Greetings. I'm so very sorry to tell you this, but you are dead . . . or rather, your body is dead."

Most ghosts don't know they are dead. They are stuck in a kind of trancelike limbo and don't realize they have lost their body. It's a revelation to most ghosts to realize that they no longer have a body. It can feel like a huge burden has lifted off them when they learn of this.

Then continue, "It's time for you to go to the light. I'm going to light a candle in your honor, and those on the other side will help you enter into the light. I wish you well on your journey." Often, you can feel the instant they leave. The candle flame will rise higher, or there will be a feeling of lightness that fills the room. It is in that moment that the ghost has indeed gone into the light.

Some people are very attached to their ghosts, especially people who are lonely. A ghost in the house feels like a kind of companion. These are not harmful situations on the whole, and sometimes there is mutual benefit. But in general, it's best for the ghost to go into the light.

Ghosts are usually easy to remove or disconnect from, unless you were very emotionally attached to that person when he was alive. In very rare cases, you might need a professional "ghost-buster." (See Chapter 2 for more information about ghosts.)

Patterns, Addictions, and Obsession Strands

A curious manifestation of cord attachments is when there is a cording to an addictive pattern, habit, or obsession. There is an energetic field for every addiction, and if you are plugged into one, it's difficult not to be influenced by it. The challenge is that once you are hooked into the collective frequency of a pattern, the energy that flows to you from the field increases within you . . . and then flows back to the collective energy field to pick up more energy, and then back to you again. It becomes a vicious cycle, which is why it's so hard to stop when there is an addictive pattern, habit, or obsession. These are some of the most important energy strands to remove . . . and if you don't, they drag you into unproductive, repetitive behaviors.

These kinds of strands can occur with any kind of unhealthy attachment to things, such as to food, drugs, alcohol . . . or even to a person. If you are obsessing about something someone did or said in the past, and you keep replaying it over and over, or you keep obsessively looking at their Facebook site, driving by their home, or checking your phone to see if they texted or called, you probably have an obsessive strand attached to that person. (If someone is doing this in regard to you, they have an unhealthy strand planted into *your* energy field.)

Is there is a food that you know is not good for you, but you keep obsessing about it, and then when you eat it—even though your mind is rebelling against you for doing so—you continue to eat more and more? This might mean that you have an obsessive strand plugged into that food frequency. (Yes, we can have energy strands connecting us to certain kinds of food.)

Unhealthy patterns of behavior and obsessive and addictive strands are some of the most difficult to remove. They often require much more than a cord-cutting ceremony. They require you going into a deep meditative state to find where the cord is attached and then notice the memories and events within yourself that are connected to it. The next step is to go into each of those events to cord-cut. These kinds of cords are often interwoven with other strands, so if you cut a cord but don't go to the source of the original cord that it is attached to, they will come back almost immediately. (See Chapter 2 for a deeper understanding of the origin of your strands.)

Here's an example of how this works: Brianna called me because she was obsessing about an ex-boyfriend. She said, "Denise, I can't stop. I know I shouldn't, but I feel like a stalker. I drive by his house; I try to see what he's doing on Facebook. I think about him all the time. I know Tim won't call me, but I check my phone over and over to see if he has called. I take out photos of the two of us and look at them all the time. I didn't even like him that much, but when he broke up with me, I was devastated. I tried cutting the cords, but it didn't work. I need help."

In a private session later, Brianna went on a relaxed meditative journey in which she found the "Tim strand" and followed it deep inside herself. She was astounded by the memories that she found glued onto the strand. When Brianna was nine years old, her father abandoned the family. It was devastating for her. She never heard from him again. She thought of her dad all the time (and even worried that it was her fault that he left).

Even though she had gotten older and didn't often think of her father, the strands remained in her energy field. So when Tim broke up with her, it was an echo of her father leaving her. The Tim strand had intertwined with her father strand, so cutting the Tim strand wouldn't be enough. In her meditation, she worked on cutting any unhealthy cords with her father.

You can keep a relationship but clear any negative cords. Just because you release a depleting cord with someone doesn't mean you no longer have a relationship with that person. It just means the negative strand flowing between the two of you no longer depletes you. This is valuable to know, especially in regard to family relationships.

A week later, Brianna called me. "Denise, it's amazing! I didn't do anything to release Tim, but I have hardly thought of him this last week. Whatever that obsession was, it's completely gone. Releasing my unhealthy dad strands in the meditation seems to have cleared the energy between Tim and me. I feel so much lighter. Thank you!"

So if you are trying to clear any kind of addictive or obsessive strands, you may need to go deeper to the original strand—and clear that one first.

Healer/Therapist/Teacher/Doctor Strands

If you are a healer or a massage therapist, you probably have had the experience of working on someone who had a particular ache or ailment, and after you worked on her, she left without it

. . . and you seemed to have gotten it. Gina was a successful massage therapist who came to me because she seemed to be absorbing all the pains and ailments of her clients. She said, "Denise, they all leave feeling so good and so happy, and I feel drained and seem to be experiencing their ailments."

This often occurs because the client forms a strong cord attachment to the healer. The loving energy of the healer flows into the client, and the pain of the client can then flow back into the healer. This same kind of attachment can occur between a client and a therapist, teacher, spiritual mentor, or doctor. If you are in a helping profession, and you feel your energy dip after working with your clients, you may want to learn how to immediately release strand attachments, so you don't take on any imbalances.

It's very important to know that if you take on an ailment or a condition from a client, or even if you absorb something from a friend or acquaintance, it is *not* the fault of the other person. *Do not blame them.* It is not their fault. (You wouldn't absorb it unless there was some kind of vibration match within you.) If there is any fault—and there isn't—it is your view of that person as unwell or as un-whole.

When we have deep sympathy for the ills or misfortunes of others, it's not uncommon to absorb their conditions into ourselves. This most likely occurs because you are a kind and sympathetic person. However, it also means that you are seeing your client, friend, or acquaintance as their disease and misfortune . . . rather than seeing the whole, majestic, remarkable being that they are. If you instead see the other person as *not* sick or *not* out of sorts but as a glorious, strong being—and interact with them as such—you won't take on stuff from them. Additionally, when you treat that individual as if they are whole, strong, and well, it is a call for them to remember who they are, and step into more vitality. If you treat someone as if they are sick or disadvantaged, that is how they tend to see themselves, and it can become a self-fulfilling prophecy.

Mantras, Chants, and Prayers Strands

Anytime you say a prayer, such as the Lord's Prayer, or chant the Sanskrit word *om*, a strand unfurls and connects you to the collective unconscious of the prayer or chant. Everyone who has said a specific prayer or chanted a particular mantra increases the vibrancy and life force of the collective energy. *The more people who chant a mantra or say a prayer, the stronger the life force of that prayer becomes.* This is one of the reasons why ancient chants are so powerful. An incredible wellspring of energy has been created by thousands (and even millions) of people, which in turn creates a profound energy loop. So when you chant *om namah shivaya*, for example, this energy surges on a cord from you to the collective; then there is a potent surge of energy and light from the collective back to you. My first teacher, the Hawaiian kahuna I mentioned in the Preface, told me there was a commanding collective of light and energy associated with the Lord's Prayer that was healing and protective. She wasn't a traditional Christian, but she had a remarkable ability to perceive energy and encouraged me to repeat the Lord's Prayer. Interestingly, my Cherokee grandparents often said the Lord's Prayer, but in Cherokee. They also said it had a majesty and grace.

Strands and Your Chakras

Strings, strands, or filaments of energy can attach anywhere throughout the body, but the most common place on your body for cords to attach is your chakra centers. Chakras are the energy centers of your body. They are aligned with various aspects of your life. For example, the chakra center in the middle of your chest is called the heart chakra. This chakra is aligned with matters of the heart. Strings of energy regarding relationships, love connections, lovers, and emotions regarding family are often attached to the heart chakra. When you are working to understand and explore the strands of energy that connect you to the world around you, it's valuable to know a bit about your chakras and the kind of cords that can attach to the various areas.

Here is a list of the chakras and the cords that commonly attach to these areas.

First chakra. This is the energy center at the base of your spine. This is called your grounding cord and your root chakra. It connects you to the earth and to your physical aspect of self. It supports you in your physical strength and in activating your survival instincts when needed. It is here that sexual cords can attach, especially from traumatic events. It can also be the place where a needy partner might attach. It's also not uncommon for small children to have attachments here; it's a place of grounding and connecting to the earth mother for them. It's a kind of energetic home base for them. Additionally, anyone who is trying to control or manipulate you might have cords here.

Second chakra. This energy center is about halfway between your navel and your root chakra; it's sometimes called the sacral chakra, although it's higher than your sacrum. Emotions from others often attach here, as well as general emotions and feelings in respect to those around you. This can include emotions regarding lovers. Also, it's common for emotional attachments to groups—religious, spiritual, or political—to reside here. Ancestral groups and familial ties often connect here.

Third chakra. This is the energy center near your solar plexus, which is called the solar chakra. This energy center often has the most attachments on the body, as it is connected to fear. Any overriding, submerged, or ongoing low-grade fear you have regarding a person or a situation is usually attached here. Also, if you don't have stellar self-esteem, this is often the easiest area for negative attachments to slip through your protective barrier and glom onto your body.

Fourth chakra. This energy center, which is located in the middle of your chest, is often called the heart chakra; love connections often attach here. This is usually a good thing, unless there is imbalance in the love connection. Often, healers and spiritual teachers have attachments here from their patients and their students. When this chakra becomes jammed, it's difficult for love to flow smoothly. There can also be a feeling of hopelessness that occurs from cords attached here.

Fifth chakra. This energy center is called the throat chakra because it is in the center of the lower part of your throat. It is concerned with communication, that is, not communicating what is in your heart, or communicating too much inappropriately. If someone is suppressing your ability to communicate, there is often an energy attachment to this chakra flowing from them to you. When this chakra is clogged, it's almost impossible to speak your truth and voice your concerns.

Sixth chakra. Called the third-eye chakra, this center is associated with your intuition and your ability to sense the unseen realms. If someone wants to "get into your head," or if they desire your wisdom, the attachment usually anchors into the sixth chakra. Additionally, if you are unduly linked to someone who has passed on, this is often where the attachment will occur.

Seventh chakra. Known as the crown chakra, this is the area that connects us to the Divine. Attachments here can be beautiful, sparkling strands of light, but there can also be attachments here from those who see you as the way to the Divine. They may want or be envious of your connection to the heavenly realms, so they will subconsciously attach here. It's important that this chakra remain clear of attachments from those who desire you to believe without discernment as they believe. These kinds of cords often come from religious leaders, teachers, political figures, and dominating individuals.

There are other places on the body where attachments occur, but the chakras or energy centers are the most common.

Celestial Strands

When I was a child, I lived with my grandparents for two years, from age nine to age twelve. My grandmother on my father's side was an astrologer; she did my chart the day I was born. She and my grandfather trained with the mystic Manly P. Hall. When I lived with her, my grandmother used to talk to me about the effect and influence of the stars on our lives. She said there were invisible lines between each of us and the stars, in accordance with their position at our birth. As a child, I used to imagine I could see these lines of light that she talked about. As an adult, I'm fascinated by our connection to the heavenly bodies.

Most of the strands connecting us to the cosmos are so thin as to be almost unrecognizable; nevertheless, we are profoundly connected to the Universe and all that is in it. We each have strands of energy that flow out to the stars, the moon, the sun, and to the vast expanse of celestial bodies. This is why astrology works. Additionally, there are strands of energy that connect us to our angels and spirit guides. These are the strands that are valuable to strengthen so that we increase the connection. (You'll be learning how to strengthen the cords that empower you in Chapter 5.)

Overlapping Strands

Sometimes energy cords are knotted together or overlapping, and trying to separate them is like undoing a tangle of yarn. When this occurs, there is an interesting dynamic. If one person sends out a strong emotion that travels along a gnarled cord, it will go to *all* the people whose cords are knotted together. So if Marsha is feeling depressed, and she has a large attachment cord to her friend Jerry and just a filament connection to Ken, who's an acquaintance, but the Jerry and Ken strands are overlapping, her depression and feeling down can go to both Jerry and Ken, because they are woven together.

Here's another example, in which tangled cords appear in the dream state: Helen had a dream about her cousin Jake, but in the dream his name was Will. He was burying bodies in the back-yard. Also at the makeshift gravesite, and kicking dirt into the grave, was Theresa, a childhood friend whom Helen hadn't been in touch with in many years. As a young girl, Theresa had contin-ually sabotaged Helen, but by all outer appearances, she seemed innocent.

The dream was disturbing and very real. When Helen began to examine it, she thought about what was occurring in her fam-ily. Her extended family (including her cousin Jake) was in an intense debate about a will left by her grandfather. Helen thought the dream reflected that there were some things that were rele-vant to the will that were being buried. She had suspected that Jake—although outwardly friendly—was the person hiding the information. (She didn't think it was an accident that Jake's name in the dream was Will.) When she thought about it, she realized that there was something similar about Theresa and Jake and the way they acted outwardly nice, but often had hidden agendas. She concluded that their strands had gotten interwoven. She noticed that after that, whenever she thought of Jake, she also thought of Theresa. They had a frequency match; hence, their strands were stuck together in Helen's mind. Chances were that any energy sent along the strand to Jake would inadvertently go to Theresa as well. Helen later found out that Jake truly was trying to "bury" some things regarding the will and he wasn't being forthright.

Collateral Strands

Sometimes strands of energy travel in a collateral way. Many years ago—before I was married—I traveled to Hawaii to visit my sister and try to recover from a challenging time in my life. I had never been to Hawaii and was excited for my journey. Before I left, a friend gave me a folded piece of paper. She said, "Denise, here is the name and phone number of my friend who lives in Hawaii. I think it would be great if you guys got together. I'm sure you have a lot in common." I thanked her and stuffed the folded piece of paper in the bottom of my purse.

I loved Hawaii. It was a joy to see my sister, and especially after the dreary darkness of winter in Michigan, the warm, sunny weather felt like heaven. As my wounded heart was healing, I found a job as a waitress at one of the pubs along the tropical shore of Waikiki. The bartender, Gary, was cute, and every time I placed an order for a cocktail, I'd joke with him while waiting for him to mix it up. Eventually, we began to date. It was fun learning about the island from his perspective. I found out where the best beaches were and which shops had great deals on jade jewelry. One day, after Gary and I had been dating for several months, I cleaned out my purse; tucked in a corner was the folded piece of paper that my friend Bridget had given me. I opened it up, and written in her flowery handwriting was Gary's full name and phone number!

This is an example of collateral strands, because Bridget was cord-connected to me and she was also corded to Gary. Gary was collateral to me, but we still connected *without knowing about each other beforehand.*

Soul Strands

There are some people we are so deeply connected to on a soul level that even if we are halfway around the world, we can feel each other through our cord connections. I met Marika many years ago when I was in London teaching at a mind-body-spirit festival. We instantly felt simpatico; it was as if we had always known each other. Wherever we went, people told us we looked like sisters. Now, this is very strange, because I'm a big woman and she is lithe. She has pale skin and red hair and I have dark hair and darker skin. She is very stylish and my style is retro hippie (and usually not too retro). She's from Finland and I'm from the United States. But when we are together, people can sense the soul connection and they think we look the same. (We actually don't at all.)

When we compared notes about our lives, it seemed a bit out of a sci-fi story because of all the similarities. For example, we both write mind-body-spirit books and we both have daughters who cook for our retreat seminars. In fact, we each have co-authored a cookbook with our daughters. We both started teaching feng-shui certification courses at the same time in our respective countries, when very few people knew what feng shui was. We both started teaching—at the same time—something that we both named "soul coaching." We both always like to have lilacs for our birthday. But it got even stranger than this, as we would discover things like that we had bought the same obscure CD on the same day and purchased the exact same shade of lipstick on the same day. The list of similarities was very long. But the strangest thing was something that occurred decades ago, before we knew each other. Marika had gone in for some blood work in Helsinki, and the doctor said, "Have you been eating a lot of papayas?" Marika replied, "No."

The doctor continued, "Well, you must be taking high doses of papain enzyme."

Marika said, "No, I've never taken papain enzyme. Why do you ask?"

With an astounded look on his face, the doctor said, "Well, the papain enzymes in your blood are very elevated, and we don't know how to account for it."

Curiously, at that exact time in my life, I was living in Hawaii. In the area where I lived, there were papaya trees everywhere, laden with the fruit for the picking. I had very little money, so I was living on papayas and mangos; consequently, my papain levels must have been very high.

Marika and I are connected on such a deep soul level that even though we live thousands of miles away from each other, our cord connection is so strong that information and wisdom travels between us almost instantaneously. There may be people on the planet with whom you share soul strands also. You may meet them or you may never come in contact with them, but the connections are so strong that they can be felt through time and space.

Computer and Social Media Strands

A modern kind of cording exists within the realm of the Internet. You can have connecting strands to Facebook friends whom you have never met in person. Thus, it's a good idea to make sure your social media friends are people with whom you feel good. The e-mails that come into your computer (and stay in your archives) can be connected to you by thin strands of energy. Are there e-mails that don't feel good that you can eliminate? If you have saved phone messages from people with whom you have cut cords, those messages will continue to reconnect you to the frequency of those people. By keeping the messages, you are keeping a bit of their energy. The people you have in your address list, even if you don't often think about them, are connected to you by strands of energy. Is there anyone with whom you have a less-than-positive association in your address book? If so, it might be a good idea to delete them from your list.

Strands to the Objects in Your Home

You can have cords connecting you to objects as well as to people, animals, and plants. Someone who won't leave their home even though a hurricane is coming has stronger cords connecting them to their home than to their body. Most of the objects in your home, and even your home itself, have strands of energy flowing between you and them.

There is indeed a secret life of inanimate objects. Have you ever noticed that your car will sometimes drive differently after someone else has taken the wheel? Or have you noticed that the washing machine or the dishwasher doesn't work the same if someone else has used it? Just as animals and plants have energy signatures, so do inanimate objects. Physical matter has the ability to absorb emotional signatures of the people around it and can even carry echoes from the past. And humans can imprint objects with their energies, even to the point of an identity emerging for the object. A machine or object that is attuned to you (and that you have ribbons of energy attaching you to) will work better for you than for other people. This is especially apparent in older machines and cars.

Your energy is also strongly connected to photos in your home, as well as to your mementos and heirlooms. If any of these have negative associations, they can bring your energy down, even if they are not on display. This is one of the many reasons why it's important to keep your home free of clutter. In Chapter 5, you'll learn more information about the impact of clutter and the objects in your home and your energy connection to them.

Sunshine Conduits

Have you noticed that there are some remarkable people around whom your energy always goes up, yet they are not depleted or drained by you or by anyone? These people are like sunshine. You don't drain the sun when you bask in its glow; you simply reflect its light. These beings are plugged into a source of energy and are conduits for sparkling, glowing strands of light and vitality. They have so many golden strands of light moving through them that it can look like sunshine is radiating out from them. Some gurus and saints are in this category, but most sunshine conduits are ordinary beings who have the ability to allow a waterfall of light to surge through them. Their fortunes can go up and their fortunes can go down, and they can have a range of emotions, yet they usually aren't diminished, because it is not their energy that continually cascades through them . . . it's a kind of universal energy that is channeled through them.

There are times when you and I are also sunshine conduits. There are times when we are connected to the source, so that all those around us are energized but we are not depleted. In fact, our energy can go up as the energy of those around us goes up, because the more that surges out of us, the more flows into us. We are indeed conduits in those moments. It feels wonderful when that happens. Sometimes we reach that place in meditation, sometimes it occurs when we are in nature and feel connected to it all, and sometimes it occurs when we are in love. It can feel like being in a state of grace. To become a sunshine conduit, one of the most important things to remember is not to take things personally.

Shielding Conduits

Just as there are some people who are channels for life-force energy, there are also people who carry a kind of shielding energy. When you are in their presence, debilitating strands of energy can't penetrate you. It is like you are under their umbrella of protection. You'll often find these kinds of people in helping professions, such as nursing, social work, emergency ward medicine, ambulance services, police work, or even prison work. They aren't wobbled by tragedies that occur around them, and they feel like a safe haven to those who are going through a hard time. Of course, this isn't true of everyone in these fields—it is only a small percentage—but you know when you are with one of these beings. They feel like a safe harbor in the storm.

Psychics often see colors associated with various energy strands and cords, and people who are shielding conduits have strands that are usually cooler in color, often steel blue and cool iridescent shades. And like the sunshine conduits, they have so many strands, it almost looks like solid color is radiating out from them. They are very rarely exhausted or diminished by those around them. The other thing they share in common with the sunshine conduits is that they don't tend to take things personally. The slings and arrows of life seem to roll off them like water off a duck's back.

Plugging into Source

The most beneficial energy strands are the ones that connect you to the greater forces of the Universe. There are many names for that force: Creator, Cosmic Consciousness, God, Goddess, Source, Great Mystery, Divine Benefactor, Universal Life Force, Mother Nature, Love, and so on. Whatever name you use for this force, it is what sustains us; it is the force that connects all things and all beings. You have a strand that connects you to that force. It might be as thin as a thread or as wide as a giant redwood tree, but you are already connected to your source. The stronger this connection becomes, the more balanced your life is. There are many ways to widen and deepen that connection strand with the creative force. For some, it's meditation or yoga; for others, it's music, painting, or dance; for others yet, it's time in nature or in retreat and solitude . . . No matter what your path is, it is worth exploring. Expanding your strands to the Creator may be the most valuable pursuit of life.

In this chapter, you have begun to learn what strands are and the kinds of strands that you might have attached to you. In the next chapter, you'll be discovering exactly which ones you have right now. You'll also discover how to scan your energy body to sense the ones that deplete you and the ones that energize you.

Chapter Two

Exploring
Your Strands

Imagine a strong woman, standing atop a hill at night under the stars. Her feet are planted solidly on the earth and her arms are raised toward the heavens. You can see lines of energy flowing out of her chakras. Some are gossamer thin and delicate—like a single strand of a spiderweb. Some are taut—almost stretched to their capacity. A few lie limp at her feet, coiled, like an ancient, forgotten rope. Others look intertwined with each other, like spaghetti. Some appear to be made of light and travel upward to the stars and moon; others reach down into the earth. Different colors and different sounds travel on each filament, ribbon, strand, or cord. Some are moving, vibrating, and undulating (as if in rhythm with the tune of an invisible band) and some seem almost solid and frozen in place. There may even be one that looks raging red and jagged; the point of insertion into her body may look raw and even woundlike.

If you were able to see the streams of energy flowing into and out of your body, what you would see would look similar to this.

You would see that you are connected to every part of the universe through your strands and filaments of energy. Most that flow into you are life-giving and wondrous. However, you might observe some that could debilitate you—like the ragged red strand into the woman on the hill. In this chapter, you'll be learning about the effects of depleting energy strands and when to take action to release these unhealthy cords. You'll also discover how to "see" your strands and learn which ones are impacting you. As you learn about negative cords and methods to recognize them, there are some things about energy to keep in mind.

Our culture's current paradigm—or way of viewing reality—is that the world is a cumbersome realm of separation. It's a place where fear and chasms between people and places rule. However, a new reality is emerging in which unity, oneness, instantaneous interconnection, and "now-ness" are blossoming. As the ravine between the old and the new shrinks, it's valuable to have a foot in each reality in order to bridge the gap. And it's important to honor each reality. Here is some information about the deeper nature of your strands.

THE DEEPER NATURE OF ENERGY STRANDS

Your strands allow you to grow. From a spiritual perspective, we are on the planet to grow, and often the way we grow is through imbalance. A plant that has to use great effort to make its way through rocky soil is often much healthier than a houseplant in a protected environment. The challenges you face in life allow you to hone and polish the facets of the gem that you are. They allow you to grow as a spiritual being. As the saying goes, "We don't learn humility from our friends." This means that it is often through disharmony that we grow the most. So instead of bemoaning the seemingly negative strands that you have, honor them and be grateful for the value you are gaining in your life through learning to deal with them. If you have strands that feel like they are diminishing you, it's valuable to recognize that they are all a part of your spiritual journey.

It's not an accident what cords are attached to you. The exact kinds of strands you have and where they have attached to you is not an accident. There is *always* a vibrational match. If you want to know what you haven't accepted in yourself, or what you judge in yourself, look at the strands that deplete you. If you want to see what you celebrate, love, and accept in yourself, examine the strands that inspire you to greater deeds and deeper love. Nothing can attach to you unless on some level there is an energy match. It is truly the law of attraction. However, if you have negative cords, there is nothing to feel guilty about; it's simply a part of the great dance of life on our planet. We all get negative strands. And we all learn from them. They are not an accident.

There is no one out there but you. In the deepest spiritual sense, there is no one out there but you. I talked about this in the introduction, but I'd like to go a bit more in depth into this.

What does it mean that there is no one out there but you? In those moments when the doctors thought I had died when I was 17 years old, I traveled to the "other side" and experienced a profound sense of oneness and unity with all things and all beings. This awareness was as natural as breathing and as true and real as anything I had ever experienced.

From my vantage point in "heaven," I "saw" that when we are on the earth plane, we feel separate from everything and everyone. We believe that others can harm us; thus, we protect ourselves from the world around us. This collective belief is so strong that when we don't protect ourselves, we *are* harmed. We believe it, and so it is true. However, this belief is an illusion. The truth is that we are all different facets of an eternal gem of light, love, and Spirit; as I mentioned before, there is nothing "out there" that can truly harm us.

The challenge is that we don't usually experience this awe-inspiring sense of oneness. There might be an occasional moment when we feel this—perhaps in meditation, or when making love, or in a heightened state of awareness. But for the most part, we are all hooked into the reality of separation. It feels so real, especially when our feelings are hurt or when someone zaps our energy. We are sure that we didn't do that to ourselves . . . someone else did it to us. How could anyone say any different? I understand this, as I also don't usually experience a feeling of oneness and grace. I usually feel separate from others and from the world around me. But the wondrous thing is that I remember the experience of knowing we are all indeed one. I don't experience it, but I remember it.

If you are like me, and you are not generally experiencing a kind of heavenly unity, but you *act* as if we are not separate from each other, your life will begin to change. Use your imagination to envision a vast, unified field of life. Over time, you will begin to realize that all strands—both the ones you perceive as negative and the ones you perceive as positive—are all part of you, and that negative strands can reflect qualities you haven't owned, loved or embraced.

This doesn't mean you shouldn't cut cords; you should. This doesn't mean you shouldn't protect yourself; you should. But it is valuable to know that those cords really are a reflection of something within you. When you realize that you are no less the mountain and the oak tree than you are your body, and when you realize that every person you meet is not just a part of you but also a part of a more expanded sense of self, you begin to understand the deeper nature of life.

We don't always remember our spiritual source, and we often forget who we are, so this chapter is for those times you forget. It will also give you an understanding of why and when to clear your strands.

SYMPTOMS OF HEAVY CORDING

There are often symptoms that go along with any depleting strands that are hooked into you. Of course, there can be many reasons for these symptoms, but sometimes there is someone or something that is sucking your energy. Go through the following symptoms and see if any apply to you.

Chronic exhaustion. Sometimes exhaustion can come from overwork, lack of sleep, unhealthy food, or doing something you don't like to do. But sometimes the exhaustion you are feeling is from debilitating strands that are attached to you, through which your life-force energy is being sucked. If you are constantly exhausted and you can't find a physical reason for it, it might be that someone or something is filtering off your energy. Most often—if it is a person—they are not consciously aware that they are doing it. Sometimes this can be temporary; for example, a friend might be going through a crisis and be subconsciously siphoning energy from you. But sometimes there is a strong negative cord anchored into you that has been draining off your life force for a long time.

Patterns that aren't yours. Sometimes the way you feel or react to a situation comes from another person. For example, Phillip was looking for a new apartment to rent, and when the real estate agent showed him a sunny, empty apartment, he suddenly felt depressed; he thought of all the things in his life that weren't going well. He even began to feel that his life wasn't worth living, and maybe he should end it all.

It surprised him to have these thoughts, because he usually was a very upbeat kind of person. When he got back home that evening, the pall and depression still hung heavy over him. He decided to use some of the techniques you will be learning in this chapter to see if there was a kind of attachment. After he did an inner journey, he felt something had attached to him when he was in the apartment, so he took steps to clear it. Afterward, he felt lighter and like his normal self.

The next morning, Phillip called the agent and said, "Can you tell me about the last person who lived in the apartment?" The agent was quiet and then reluctantly answered, "He died suddenly."

Phillip persisted, "I'm sorry for asking, but I'd like to know how he died."

Again, the agent was hesitant, but he finally said, "I heard that he was very depressed . . . and committed suicide."

Phillip realized that the pattern of depression of the previous occupant still clung to the apartment . . . and had attached to him. He told me he was lucky he recognized that the depression wasn't his and was able to release it.

Sue, a massage therapist who attended one of my seminars, told me that she had a good example about someone adopting a pattern of behavior because of an energy attachment. She said that she was always a very trusting person; in fact, family members and friends used to constantly comment about how trusting she was.

Then, almost overnight, she began to be fearful. She started to triple check the doors each time she left the house, to make sure that she had locked them. Sometimes she would even drive back home to see if she had actually locked the doors. She also began to check and recheck her purse to make sure that her wallet was still in it.

Sue said that the pattern of behavior just didn't seem like her. When she was chatting with a new client, he mentioned that he always checked and rechecked his home and car, worried that he had forgotten to lock the car. Sue realized her pattern of behavior had started right after she began to work with that particular client. The pattern wasn't hers; it had filtered through the strand that connected the client to her. As soon as she released the strand, she no longer worried about locking doors. She told me that she kept the client, but just established healthy energy barriers so that he was in his energy . . . and she was in hers.

Here's another example that happened while I was in Mexico teaching a dream workshop: At the dinner break, a woman sat down next to me and proceeded to tell me that she never could sleep. She listed all the supplements and drugs she was taking to get some sleep, and yet nothing worked. She said that she had a hard time getting to sleep and then she woke up often during the night. I had immense sympathy for her; it's awful not to be able to get a good night's sleep. Just as I was about to go to sleep that night, I thought of her and sent her love. In my life, it's rare that I can't get to sleep immediately, but that night I lay in bed . . . watching the clock. (Usually I'm asleep within 30 seconds of closing my eyes. My husband is in awe of my ability to drop off to sleep so quickly.)

After a few hours, I finally drifted off, only to wake 30 minutes later. Then, for most of the remainder of the night, I was up about every half hour. Finally, early in the morning, I tried to understand what was happening, as it was so unusual. Suddenly, the face of the woman who couldn't sleep came into my mind. I realized that in our chat, I had formed an energy strand with her . . . and her sleeplessness became my sleeplessness. I used the "wrap, pull, and ground" method that you will find on page 105 in Chapter 3 and finally was able to sleep for the remaining hours.

Random unwanted thoughts. We all have millions of thoughts zipping throughout our brains every day. Almost all of these thoughts are our own. We can have random thoughts that are seemingly unacceptable to us, and other random thoughts that are in alignment with how we see ourselves. This is the nature of thoughts.

Sometimes, however, a random thought doesn't originate in your brain; it is the result of a strand between you and another. Someone will think of you, and the thought travels on the strand between you and them. You may wake up with a random thought about someone, or someone you haven't thought of for a long time may show up in a dream. In my life, those random thoughts usually tell me when someone is thinking of me. I love it. It's a kind of psychic telephone system, keeping us in touch with each other. These thoughts are often heartfelt. If someone I haven't thought of for a long time pops into my random thoughts, I usually call them or e-mail them, and almost always that individual says they were thinking of me with love. This is one of the mysterious and wondrous things I deeply enjoy about life.

There are times, however, when random thoughts can be disturbing, and this can be indicative of someone thinking of you in a less-than-positive way. They can be negative thoughts that have traveled through a strand from another person to you.

Hazel, one of my students, shared an experience that she felt was an unwanted random thought from another. She said that, seemingly out of the blue, she had a thought about poisoning her cats. She was profoundly and overwhelmingly shocked and upset by the thought. She loved her cats. They were her life companions and she cherished them with a passion. The thought deeply distressed her.

Then a few days later, the random thought emerged again. She was visibly shaken by it. As a result, she decided to keep her cats in, rather than letting them out in the yard. She told me that the second time it came up, she knew it wasn't *her* thought. But she didn't understand where it was coming from. However, not long after that, her next-door neighbor was arrested for poisoning cats in the neighborhood. Hazel realized that probably he had attached a strand to her and his thoughts about her cats were traveling through the strand to her. She picked them up, *but at first they seemed like her thoughts.*

Here's another example of how this works: I was having lunch with a client, and in the course of our conversation, I casually asked her about her ex-husband. She said she didn't ever think of him and hadn't heard from him in four years. The next afternoon, however, she heard from her son that her ex had called him, asking about her *at the same time we had been talking about him.* (He hadn't called to talk to her son for several years.) She realized that she must still have cords connecting to him, and he must have picked up on her talking about him . . . and that's why he called. She felt it was time to do more cord cutting.

Emotions that you can't seem to control. Sometimes a cord attachment will cause you to experience emotions that you don't seem to have any control over. Jeannette was our neighbor when we lived on the central coast of California. She called me one night in a panic. An acquaintance of hers was in an abusive marriage, and when things escalated with her husband, she called Jeanette to ask if Jeanette could drive her to a women's shelter where she could stay until her husband cooled off.

Jeanette didn't know this acquaintance very well and had never met the husband, but she agreed. It took a while for her friend to get checked into the shelter, but Jeanette waited until everything was settled.

About six hours later, when she was back home with her husband, whom she had been happily married to for almost 46 years, something very upsetting happened to Jeanette. She said what occurred was especially shocking because they lived a very peaceful life and in their entire married life they had had only a couple of arguments, which were resolved quickly. (My husband and I knew Jeannette and her husband . . . they were both very levelheaded, gentle, amenable people. When she said they didn't argue, I believed her.)

Jeannette told me that they had been sitting and watching a movie on television, as they did almost every night, and her husband said something inconsequential. But for some unknown reason, an uncontrollable rage ripped through Jeanette as he said it. She abruptly grabbed a large, heavy vase, and aimed it at the large living room window. Ashen-faced, her husband looked at her in shock. Nothing like this had ever happened in their decades of marriage.

Jeanette said that it took all of her willpower not to break the window. She was horrified at what had almost happened. Once she sat down and caught her breath, she remembered talking with me about energy strands, so she picked up the phone and called me.

While we talked, she realized that while she was sitting at the women's shelter, she must have picked up violent energy. She said that she felt very open and vulnerable while she was there, because she had so much sympathy for her acquaintance and for any woman who would need to resort to a shelter. She felt that a cord must have attached to her, presumably from some residual energy in the center. (Of course, others could spend time in the center without any challenges; it's just that she was very open and empathetic at that time.) I shared ways that she could unhook from it. Jeannette was so happy that she was able to understand what had happened and why, so she could prevent it in the future.

Unhealthy attachment to things, people, and places. It's natural to have attachments to people, places, and objects, but if there are too many attachments, or if they are too strong, sometimes our circuitry can get jammed, and we are not as clear about life as we could be. A person who runs into a burning home to save their jewels—to the detriment of their own life—most likely has very strong strands connecting them to their jewelry. People who live in very cluttered houses often are so attached to their objects that they can't release them, even if they don't use them or love them. And consequently, their life force becomes clogged.

Aching for a past relationship. Do you have a compulsion to go back to a past relationship? Do constant memories concerning things you used to do together play over and over again in your mind? Someone who is no longer in a relationship but pines obsessively for that person, without abatement, or endlessly processes the past, may have very strong cords to that person. Someone who is constantly checking their phone to see if a particular someone called, or is stalking them on Facebook, or driving by their house to see if they are home . . . usually has unhealthy attachment strands. Sometimes obsessive cord attachments can throw the person that they are focused on into turmoil; however, if the individual has a strong energy field, it won't be a challenge for them.

Do you keep trying to leave a relationship, but every time you feel that you have cut it off, the person somehow pops back into your life? Perhaps someone in your life is clingy and dependent on you, and yet you can't seem to release the relationship. Is there someone you're afraid of bumping into, or do you screen your calls and texts because you're avoiding certain people? Do you start coughing or choking when you are around a particular person? These can all be indicative of unhealthy cord attachments.

Some cord attachments can go beyond death. When someone dies, sometimes we can't let go, and the cord remains strong. This can be a wonderful way to stay connected to a beloved who has passed on, but in some cases, the person on earth is not present in their life because part of their life force is focused on the dead person. These kinds of strands can also keep a spirit earthbound, so they can't go to the light.

Obsessive thoughts. Do you replay an incident from the past again and again? Do hurtful incidents from childhood keep emerging, sometimes without warning? Do you hold on to anger, resentment, or bitterness for something that someone said or did, even though it is in the far past? And do you review these events again and again? Do you continually turn down invitations from friends and family because you are stuck replaying the past?

If you answered yes to any of these questions, your obsessive thoughts are often indications of strong negative strand attachments.

Repetitive conversations with someone in your head. Do you keep replaying part of a conversation again and again, obsessing about what you said or what they said? Do you keep having repetitive conversations with someone in your head?

If you are continually ruminating on things someone said, thinking about what you wish you had said, or incessantly reliving the judgment or criticism you think someone has about you, chances are there are fear-based cords between you and the other person.

Plotting ways to get revenge. Do you fervently wish that the guy who cut you off in traffic would get a speeding ticket at the next bend? Do you constantly think about the negative Yelp review you are going to write about someone or something? Do you imagine ways you can get back at someone for the wrong she did you? Have you visualized writing an anonymous letter to the boss so he really knows what's going on in the office? Do you sometimes not only visualize what you would like to do to someone but actually take action on it? All right, then: you have some heavy-duty cords between you and that other person.

Please do not judge yourself harshly if you fall into this category. People who think about getting back at someone who wronged them usually are people who subconsciously feel that they don't have personal power. You'll know you are stepping into your power when these kinds of thoughts begin to recede.

Sympathy pains. Have you ever been around someone who tells you about how bad their headache is, and shortly afterward, you get a whopping headache? Sarah went to the hospital to visit her friend who'd had her gallbladder surgically removed. When she left, Sarah had severe pain in her gallbladder area. People who get "sympathy pain" are usually compassionate and kind beings. They can feel the sufferings of the world, and they have deep compassion for those in pain. The challenge is that these kinds of people often have so many cords attaching them to those they have empathy for, their energy system is overloaded. They literally do take on the pain of the world.

Depression and hopelessness. Of course, these kinds of emotions can come from many things, but they can also indicate that your energy has been filtering away to someone or something for a long period of time. This can even be an ancestral strand. Gordon had an uncle, Tom, who he was very attached to. Uncle Tom had always been Gordon's support during his life and especially during his traumatic childhood. However, during the later years of Tom's life, he became depressed and despondent.

After Tom's death, Gordon was depressed. He thought it was because he missed his uncle. But the feelings continued. He went into therapy and still couldn't seem to shake a feeling of hopelessness. It was only when he examined his strands and saw that the biggest one was connected to his uncle that he understood what had happened. He was feeling and absorbing his uncle's depression. He remembered that I had said you can keep a relationship but still release the negative strands that flow between you and another; so that's what he did.

Gordon said he felt a huge weight lift from him as soon as he did that. He contacted me six months later and said that it felt like a miracle. He hadn't had any depression since he had released the strands. It had simply vanished.

These are all symptoms of heavy cording, or having strands that are dragging you down or depleting you. The next step is to figure out when you should take action.

WHEN SHOULD YOU TAKE ACTION?

You've now learned some of the effects of unhealthy attachments. In this next section, you'll discover when you should take action to release strands. If left unattended, energy attachments can grow over time, so you should clear your energy when you are drained from:

- Energy vampires
- Psychic attacks
- Possession
- "Toxic" people
- Dream stompers
- Sadness, fear, anger, and other emotions that are not yours
- Grief recovery after the death of a loved one
- Residual and predecessor energy from a home or workplace
- Groups such as religious, spiritual, or political organizations that are not love based

Energy Vampires . . . Are They Real?

One of the most important times to take action is if you feel constantly drained and exhausted around someone who is in your life on a consistent basis. Over time, this will have a debilitating effect on you and your health and well-being. There can be many reasons for this feeling of fatigue. Most of the time, when your energy lags when you are in proximity to someone else, it is simply a mismatch of energy fields in that moment. It's nothing to be concerned about.

However, there are some people who always seem to sap everyone around them—no matter where they go and no matter who they are around. Often, they are the kind of person that constantly seeks approval. You may notice that when they hug you, they desire multiple hugs, or they hold on for a few seconds past your comfort level. They often want to express their emotions and constantly talk about their problems to you. They seem perky and revitalized afterward . . . and you feel drained. While it is important to be compassionate and listen with an open heart, if you feel yourself becoming incredibly exhausted, it may be that there is some "vampire-y" energy afoot and you may need to pull your energy in. (I don't like the term *energy vampire*, as it seems highly judgmental, but I use it because this may be the way the energy dynamic feels to you. You may feel that your life force is being sucked out of you. It describes how *you* may feel, rather than being a judgment of another person.)

Almost always, these kinds of people have no idea that they are responsible for your energy drain. *These are not bad people*; they are usually people who don't feel that there is enough energy and love available for everyone. They often feel that they can't get enough love (or don't deserve it). They don't trust that they can fulfill their own needs, and as a result, they subconsciously believe that the only way their need for energy can be met is to take energy from others. These kinds of submerged thoughts diminish their life vitality and they become weakened. These individuals are stuck in a feeling of desperate neediness, and they don't realize that they have the capacity to tap into their own wellspring of energy. We should have compassion for energy vampires; they usually don't have any true friends, and whatever fleeting relationships they have don't usually last long because their partners get drained and tired.

After my large seminars, it's not uncommon for someone to come up, give me a big hug, and say, "Here, I'm going to give you some energy!" In almost every single case, not only have I *not* received energy, but my energy was diminished. The hugger, however, left feeling really good, because they believed that they had done a good deed. Of course, I don't fault these individuals. In their mind, they think they are giving energy and they believe they did a good deed. (They would be shocked to know that they took energy. They just don't know any better.)

There is often drama around people who are severe energy vampires, which means everyone around them focuses on them, which in turn means there is more energy for them to draw on. Energy vampires will sometimes pit people against each other because of the energy they receive when someone sides with them. It's not uncommon for them to be involved in arguments and even launch seemingly unfair emotional attacks on others, all with the subconscious goal of generating emotional energy they can hook into. They can tangle your words and turn them against you in unfair ways, especially words that you shared when you were feeling vulnerable. They usually need to be right in every situation and they lack the ability to see the points of view of others. They constantly seem to be declaring, "I'm right and you are wrong." They have to be right, at any cost.

One of the signs of an energy vampire is that they don't trust people; there is often a sense of paranoia around them, and they can sometimes seem hypervigilant. It can feel as if they are waiting for someone to disagree with them or judge them, so they can lash out and make a scene. This creates drama, enabling them to suck energy out of the situation.

They can often be seen as perfectionists, but the need to control their environment belies a feeling of lack of control within themselves. Strangely, they often think that others are draining their energy, so they respond by draining the energy of those around them. (I've found that many of the people who come to me complaining that they are the victims of energy vampires are, in fact, the ones who are draining energy off others.)

One of the most common qualities of energy vampires is that they act like they are helpless victims of life. They talk incessantly about how unfair life has been to them and they constantly are needy, demanding help. The challenge is that those who try to help—and enter into the role of the rescuer—get more and more drained, since nothing is ever enough.

Have you ever known someone who threatened to quit or leave a project or a situation, but in reality wasn't going to leave? They just wanted you to try to talk them out of it. This is another way an energy vampire saps your energy. They get their juice by the energy you put out to talk them into staying.

Also, they try to use guilt to manipulate others to give them energy. For example, an energy vampire might say, "You didn't leave the keys for the company car when you left work . . . and I had to get a taxi, and the taxi didn't have a heater and I got a terrible chill and the smell in the cab was so bad that I had an allergic reaction . . . so none of the reports are ready for you." As a result, the energy vampire feels powerful and righteous, and subconsciously wants you to feel bad, forcing an apology, which results in even *more* energy for the energy vampire.

Are narcissists, passive-aggressive people, and "martyrs" energy vampires? Usually narcissists fit the category of being energy vampires, as well as passive-aggressive people and the long-suffering martyrs. Martyrs are people who sometimes do nice things—that were never asked for—and then get resentful when they aren't appreciated to the extent that they desire. Or they offer to do nice things, but then get resentful if you actually accept. People who are passive-aggressive can also be energy drainers. They will say something supportive, but then do things to undermine you.

In all relationships, there is a giving and taking of energy; sometimes one person may give more, and other times they may receive more. This is a natural ebbing and flowing of energy. The kind of strand that can deplete you is a connection to someone around whom *you always feel drained*. Being with these kinds of people—and even just thinking of them—can be incredibly draining and exhausting; they are a kind of energy vampire.

The Law of Attraction and Vampires. Are you thinking of some people who have been in your life who may have been energy vampires? Before pointing your finger at those in your life whom you suspect, examine the law of attraction. If you have been a "victim" of an energy vampire, there is the possibility (and even likelihood) that something in you attracted them and that, on some level, you share the same vibration. Energy vampires are often attracted to those who don't have personal boundaries or who lack personal power. (A personal boundary doesn't mean you have a wall around yourself. It simply means you don't demean yourself in pursuit of the approval of others.)

Do you need to examine your boundaries in life? Do you constantly resent the actions of others? Do you frequently feel treated in an unfair manner? If you answer yes to these questions, or if you put the needs of others far above your own or don't share your truth for fear of being rejected, this can leave you open to being sucked dry by an energy vampire.

We may fling judgments at energy vampires, such as that they are the kind of people who can't stand on their own two feet, so they have to take strength from others. However, if there are some of these energy vampires in your life, examine yourself to see if you might also share their subconscious belief. Do you subconsciously feel that you don't have enough strength, vitality, or love . . . and there just isn't enough to go around? If so, there could be a frequency match between you and your energy vampires. It might be time to shift the way you perceive yourself and your life. Energy vampires feed off weakness and fear. To stop them, step into personal empowerment, courage, and grace, and they will drop away.

If there is an energy vampire in your life or people you feel almost comatose around after being in their presence, consider shielding before encountering them. (Or better yet, avoid them whenever possible.) See Chapter 4 for highly effective shielding and protection methods.

Psychic Attacks

Psychic attacks are real. They are different from being drained by an energy vampire, because vampires suck energy out of you. A psychic attack can come from someone who is consciously (or subconsciously) and deliberately wishing you harm. It is direct and can be very disturbing. It is similar to someone slugging you in the stomach, but it is done with energy. To find out more about these kinds of attacks, and how to protect yourself from them, see Chapter 4.

Possession

Another time to take action is in the case of possession. (Possession is when a spirit occupies or shares a body with someone.) This is a kind of internal cording. There is a strong cord between someone and the spirit of a departed person who has entered their body. There are writings about possession going back to the earliest human history. In my original training, my Hawaiian kahuna taught me how to release ghosts—which could also be called earthbound spirits—and she also trained me to release spirits from people who were possessed. She said it was very rare to encounter a possession, but she wanted me to be prepared.

In those early days, many people came to me regarding ghosts that needed to be released. It was a bit like Hollywood—when ghosts were released, doors would bang, windows would slam shut, and lights would go on and off. (Later, I realized that I subconsciously relished the drama, but I didn't know that at the time. What you focus on is what you draw to you.) One day, during the time in my life when I was releasing ghosts, someone came to me because she believed she was possessed; she had good reason to think this. I went to her home and released the spirit as I had been taught. The woman felt overjoyed that the entity had left her.

I didn't know if it was a true possession or not, as most are psychological and imaginary. But when I left her home and went to out to my car, which I had left parked in front of her home, I couldn't find it. It wasn't there. I had locked it, and I had locked the wheels. I was puzzled. Then I noticed my car half a block away; it was up on someone's lawn. The wheels were still locked and the car was still locked, yet it was 100 feet away. Either a football team of hefty guys had lifted my car and carried it down the road, or something supernatural had occurred.

I still don't know for sure what happened, but as I looked at my displaced car, I realized it was time to stop focusing on ghosts and possession. After that, they were simply off my radar. And over the next 48 years that I have been teaching, I have encountered only a few ghosts and one possession. As soon as I stopped focusing on ghosts, I no longer had ghosts to clear and I almost never ran into any. What you focus on is what you attract into your life.

The one possession I mentioned occurred when I was teaching in Australia. It was the midday break for the very large event that I was teaching. I was anxious to get to lunch, but the line of folks wanting to talk to me or have me sign a book was long. Two women came up to me. One looked pale and dazed. She said, "My friend is possessed. I'm scared, because she tried to drive us off the road yesterday."

I knew that only rarely is there true possession—almost always, the symptoms are psychological—so I wasn't concerned. Sometimes people get a feeling of being important by imagining they are possessed. Or others subconsciously try to get sympathy from the drama created because they are a victim of someone they believe is possessed.

So, nonchalantly, I said, "Okay. Let's get that pesky spirit out of there."

I didn't think to protect myself, because I didn't think there was anything to protect against. I didn't really think the woman was possessed. I wouldn't have been so cavalier if I had thought it was a true possession (and I really wanted to get to lunch).

I told the woman I was going to thump her chest fairly hard, and when I did, the "spirit" would leave her. I made my hand into a loose fist, counted, "One, two, three!" and shouted "Out!" as I thumped her chest.

She jolted; the stress lines around her mouth and forehead had smoothed. Her eyes were clear. Looking astonished and relieved, she exclaimed, "It's gone! It's gone! Thank you! Oh my God, it's gone!"

I assumed that she had released the *belief* that she was possessed, and then I forgot about it, and went on to answer a question from the next person in line. Finally, the last person left. As I turned to gather my purse, I suddenly began to have severe muscle contractions. It felt like my entire body was constricted, as if I were having a seizure. I fell onto the carpet, convulsing. The promoter was shocked. "What's happening? Should I get a doctor?"

I could hear his words, but they seemed muffled and far away, as if I were at the end of a long, dark tunnel. I frantically thought, *What's happening?* Suddenly, I knew. *The woman* was *possessed and the entity jumped off her onto me.* Damn.

The promoter was leaning over me. I whispered, "Possession."

He had seen me thump the woman and tell her the entity was gone, so he knew what I was talking about. He grabbed a piece of paper and frantically drew the Star of David on it. (He was Jewish and believed the Star of David would protect me.) He was shoving it in my mouth, trying to get me to swallow it to clear me of the entity. I was worried this was going to choke me.

As everything was getting darker and darker, I saw a pinpoint of light receding in front of me. As the light continued to shrink, I heard an inner voice say, *Remember who you are.*

Simply said, those words changed everything.

Remember who you are.

To myself I thought, *I am all that is and ever will be. There is nothing that is not me. I am infinite. The Creator dwells within me . . . as me. There is only grace and love.*

With these words, the pinpoint of light became brighter and brighter . . . until I was flooded with radiant, shimmering, golden light. In that moment, I knew that there was no entity and no possession. Whatever had attached to me was gone . . . only light remained.

Remembering who I was had made the difference. Even though I insisted that recalling my true nature had changed everything, the promoter was sure that swallowing the Star of David had done the trick. (I *had* actually managed to chew it up and swallow it, at his insistence!) I have respect for the Star of David, but I knew this wasn't what had cleared the entity. But I thanked him anyway for his quick thinking. We went to lunch and on to the rest of the seminar, and there was no residue from the experience.

I was torn about telling you this story, because I didn't want to incite fear within you about possible possessions. (And I can almost guarantee a true possession will never happen to you or around you. It is so very uncommon.) However, I decided to share it, in the very rare event that you encounter possession. And if you do, remember who you are. It's that simple. You are a majestic, sparkling being of light. You don't need any special words to recite. This method applies not just to so-called possession, but also to any challenge in life. When you remember who you are, and when you remember that you are an infinite being of grace, love, and light . . . there is no room for anything else. You are not a victim of life, nor do you need to be.

"Toxic" People

Sometimes you may have people who you consider toxic in your life. If so, you should immediately take action to de-cord them from your energy field. These are people who deplete your energy or make you feel a sense of low self-esteem after having been with them. (*The term doesn't necessarily mean that those* people *are toxic; it means that the cords flowing between you and that person are toxic to you.*) These people are not energy vampires, as they don't suck your energy, and they are not psychic attackers, as they do not consciously wish you ill. These are people whose state of mind is so negative that they seem to pollute everyone around them. On a perfectly beautiful day, they will talk about the bad weather that's coming or the amount of pollen in the air. Someone might compliment their new haircut and they will complain about how much it cost them or the awful smell they had to endure in the salon. No matter what topic comes up, they find a way to take a negative slant on it. They are just simply and utterly negative in their approach to life. What's crazy is that the only thing that seems to make them happy is if someone else is negative alongside them . . . and they can complain together.

It's hard not to judge someone who is always negative and always complaining. However, your judgment about another can damage you. I know it's hard to do when you are around someone who is so wearisome, but rather than harshly judging that person, have compassion for them. (No one really wants to go around depleting other people's energy—they just want to be loved and accepted, but they don't know how to go about it.) Know that simply because they are toxic to you doesn't mean that they are toxic in general. Their soul is not toxic. Some people are allergic to strawberries or to shrimp. It's not that strawberries or shrimp are necessarily toxic; it's just that they are toxic to some people.

Dream Stompers

Dream stompers are different from other kinds of energy depleters; they are usually well-meaning, loving people. Yet if you have a dream stomper in your life, it might be time to cut the cord—or at least the strand that carries their diminishing energy. Usually, dream stompers are kindhearted people; often, they are people who are close to you or they are family members. Under the guise of protecting you, they will judge and demean your dreams. They will say that it's not going to be possible for your dream to come true because you don't have the skills, the money, the time, or the education, or because of any number of logical reasons. And they might be right—you might not have the money, skill, education, intelligence, or time—and they think they are saving you from failure or disappointment. But in truth, they are killing the spark of innovation and inspiration for you to go forward with your dreams. These are some of the hardest cords to purge, as these people consciously want the best for you. They feel like they are protecting you from hardship. It's hard not to listen to them, as they are often the closest to you in your life and they declare that they want the best for you.

I know about dream stompers. My high school guidance counselor advised me not to go to college. She said that, instead, I should focus on getting a husband and becoming a homemaker. My father told me the same thing; he said that college was more for men than for women, as men were the breadwinners. (It was a strange thing to say, as my mother had multiple college degrees. She was in the first generation in her family, as far back as anyone could remember, that had a college education.) Both the guidance counselor and my father thought they were doing me a favor and thought they were helping me in my future. (I did make it to college eventually. It was not easy.) Numerous times in my life, I've been told I didn't have enough (or wasn't enough) to make my dreams come true. Yet, each time, I clicked my heels and declared to the world (and to myself) that I was enough . . . and I kept going. If you have dream stompers in your life, it's important to try to be impervious to their criticism; let things roll off your back and don't take it personally. Remind yourself that in their mind, they are helping you.

It is really hard to not listen to dream stompers, and it's even harder to have a gentle, loving amusement as they wail about how miserably you will fail. However, it is worth the effort. If you decide to do some cord cutting from the dream stompers in your life, remember that you can keep the relationship and just cleave the strand that flows to the part of you that reacts negatively when your dreams are being stomped.

Sadness, Fear, or Anger That Is Not Yours

If you consistently have emotions that are "not yours," then it's time to cut some strands. Of course, it can be all too easy to declare that your emotions aren't yours, rather than exploring your inner consciousness to see if there is something in your life or in your psyche that can account for them. But if you have searched your inner being and can't find anything to account for the emotions, then there is a chance they are not yours . . . and the strands to that person or to those people who are igniting those emotions should be severed.

Curiously, sometimes an emotion that isn't yours can be a cord attachment to a future event or to a future collective consciousness. Early on the morning of September 11, 2001, in Paso Robles, California, I was awakened by a horrific dream. A huge tree—as wide and as tall as a skyscraper—was being felled at its base by a Middle Eastern–looking man with a dark beard. Above me, people were falling out of the tree to their death. There was blood everywhere. And then the tree collapsed in on itself.

It was such a horrific dream that I got out of bed and ran out to my car without taking my pajamas off; I then drove to the top of a high hill. I needed the wide-open space atop the hill just to feel that I could breathe. I was distraught and heavy with dread. My immediate assumption was that there was something dark in my psyche that I hadn't explored; I thought that I had to do a lot of inner work to clear it. As I looked to the eastern horizon, I heard an inner voice say, *It begins today.* I assumed this meant that I needed to start doing some deep psychological work starting that very day.

Eventually, I drove back to the house, but I felt heavier and heavier. When I stepped through the door, a friend from New York called. I told her about my dream. I just couldn't shake it. We talked for about 30 minutes, and she had her television on in the background. Suddenly, she exclaimed, "Denise, oh my God! On the news, it says that a plane just now hit one of the Twin Towers!" From that point, she told me everything that was happening as she watched her television in horror. We don't have television reception, so I didn't see the images right away. A few days later—when I saw the videos and the people falling out of the tower—it was almost exactly what I had seen in my dream.

In my dream, I had unconsciously cord-attached to a future event; the trauma traveled through the cord to me, but I thought it was my "stuff." If it hadn't been for mass communication, I might have never known that the feeling of dread was regarding a future event and not something within my energy field. So, if you have unexpected emotions, it's valuable to take time to discern the source; it might be something in the future.

Grief Recovery after the Death of a Loved One

One of the most difficult things in life to deal with is the death of a loved one . . . both beloved human friends and family members as well as our animal companions. The pain of that loss can penetrate to the core of our being. It's important to grieve. And there is no set amount of time for someone to grieve. In some native cultures, the grieving time is one year. However, some people move through the grieving cycle more quickly, and other people take years. There is no right or wrong. It takes the time that it takes.

There are times, however, when you feel that you have completed your grief, yet a heaviness of heart continues. If this is the case, there may be an energy attachment to the beloved that is weighing you down. It may be time to release it . . . with love. It doesn't mean that love still doesn't flow between you—it will continue to blossom. It just means that you can get on with your life, and they can continue with their evolution in the spirit world.

Residual and Predecessor Energy from a Home or Workplace

When you move into a new environment, you may feel exhausted and unlike yourself. Of course, any change can be stressful. However, there are times when it is the residual and predecessor energy from that new locale that is depleting you. In other words, you have cord connected to the energy that preceded you and/or to the people who occupied that locale before you. If this is the case, it's very important to do a cord cutting process. In Chapter 5, I share a space clearing technique that is helpful in these situations. After the residual energy has been cleared, you might want to establish a protective shield around your space. Different ways to shield and protect your space can be found in Chapter 4.

Groups That Are Not Love Based

Another area in which it's valuable to take action to release strands of energy is in regard to groups that are not supportive or empowering for you. If you belong to a group—a religious, spiritual, political, or volunteer organization—that is not kind and loving, and you notice that your energy drops every time you participate, then it may be time to cut some cords. Dorothy told me that she had been a Baptist her entire life. Her parents, grandparents, and great-grandparents had all been Baptists. As a child, she had enjoyed going to church, but as she moved into adulthood, she noticed that every time she got back from church, she was exhausted and drained. She felt that there was nothing wrong with the Baptist beliefs, but it wasn't a match for her energy at that time in her life. Dorothy told me that when she cut the cords to the church organization, but not to the religion itself, she felt like she could breathe again. She hadn't realized how much it had weighed on her. She said the cords were very dense and large. She thought this was because of the ancestral connection to the church. It's important to remember, as Dorothy did, that you can cut the cords to an organization or group and yet maintain cords to a belief or philosophy.

INVESTIGATION AND ASSESSMENT OF YOUR STRANDS

To discover what cord attachments you have and how much they influence you, there are a few things you can do. In this section, you'll learn some methods to explore and investigate your strands. You'll also learn some visualization and dowsing techniques you can do yourself to tap into your natural knowing. The stronger your intuition, the more powerful results you will obtain in the journey to find and explore your strands. Your intuition will allow you to get a clearer understanding of what you are attached to.

To start, here are three things that are essential for activating your intuition.

Activate Your Intuition

1. Trust your intuitive sense. Although we live in a technological age that generally prizes logic and disparages intuition, there is still a part of you that is intimately connected to the invisible world of energy that is around you. Even if you have consciously forgotten this connection, you can still tap into it. Many people can sense that something is about to happen seconds before an accident. Or perhaps they receive a clear image of who is calling just as they reach to pick up the phone. Other people have these same sensations when they see a meteor shooting across the sky—a sense of wholeness, a precognitive awareness of what's really important in life. The feelings and sensations that arise within us at these times come out of the place where our inner voice speaks to us. This voice is constantly giving us guidance and information. To hear it, you must first place your *trust* in it. Even when it doesn't seem to make sense to your conscious mind, pay attention to this voice. Listen to what it is telling you. Trust it.

2. Be willing to be wrong. One of the greatest barriers to trusting your intuitive voice is your fear of being wrong. To develop your instinctive knowing, let go of your need to be right. When I teach intuition, I've noticed that the students who get the best results are the ones who don't give a hoot whether they are wrong or not. The person who is frightened of failing will subconsciously restrict the free flow of the intuitive mind.

Be willing to fail. Embrace your failures! Every time you fail, you learn something. When you are wrong, you connect with a kind of beginner's mind, the place where you are ready to learn, to listen, and to receive.

3. Practice your intuitive skills. Developing your intuition is no different from learning any other new skill. You need to practice in order to get better. There are lots of easy ways to exercise your intuition. For example, when you are waiting at traffic lights, guess how many red cars will pass going the other way before the light turns green. You won't always get it right, but when you do, *notice the feeling you have* and notice any accompanying physical sensations. Emotions and physical sensations are inner indicators that highly intuitive people use in order to find answers to their questions. George, who is highly intuitive, always gets a particular sensation in the center of his chest when his intuition is focused and clear. As you practice, you can begin to recognize what signals your body will give you.

SCAN TO FIND YOUR STRANDS

One of the most powerful exercises to discover your strands is to scan your body while in a meditative state. It is simple, yet it is the most effective method to discover your energy strands. Here's how to do this:

1. Sit or lie down somewhere where you feel very safe and very comfortable. Make sure you are warm.

2. Close your eyes and take a few very deep, relaxing breaths.

3. Imagine that your body is standing on a grassy hill but that you have stepped out of your body, so you can view it from a short distance.

4. As you observe your body, you can see filaments, threads, strands, ribbons, cords, ropes, and maybe even some thin cobwebs of energy flowing out of your chakras and out of various areas of your body. Notice their color, texture, size, temperature, and where in your body each one is attached.

5. Choose one of the strands and imagine you are touching it. If you can, gently lift it up slightly and slide your hand along the underside of it, and then imagine that you are following it back to the person, place, thing, or situation it is attached to.

6. When you come out of this meditation, consider writing down what you have discovered.

Dowse to Find Strands

Another exercise you can do to discover your strands is dowsing. Dowsing is a way to tap into your intuition. With the help of a dowsing tool, this method of prediction can help you find answers to questions, as indicated by the movement of the pendulum or dowsing rod.

A pendulum consists of a weighted body or object that swings from a fixed point. It can be a crystal, a stone, a large bead, a key, or something else that hangs from a chain or cord. You don't need to purchase a pendulum; literally anything can work. You can even make your own. If you use a necklace, all you need to do is make sure there is a stone or charm attached to it that has enough weight to allow it to swing back and forth, and you have a pendulum.

The art of dowsing has been used for thousands of years. Prehistoric rock paintings in Algeria depict early dowsers, and research has uncovered evidence suggesting that the ancient Chinese and Egyptians used dowsing. The first written descriptions of dowsing appeared in the Middle Ages. One striking example can be found in a book called *De re metallica*. This book, first published in 1556, contains a number of woodblock illustrations showing various stages of dowsing with a forked branch.

Although there are many schools of thought regarding why dowsing is successful, practitioners of this ancient art all agree on one point: it works. One explanation for why dowsing for water has been so successful over the centuries is that the dowser is able to detect subtle electromagnetic fields emanating from underground water. There may be a scientific foundation for this theory, because flowing water does create a natural electrical field. However, this idea fails to explain why other forms of dowsing work.

Many believe that dowsing works because dowsers subconsciously tune in to the stream of wisdom accessible at the level of the collective unconscious of all people. The dowser receives information from this source, causing muscles to twitch, which in turn causes the rod to turn or the pendulum to swing. In other words, the body of the dowser becomes a receiving station for a flow of energy. The dowsing tool acts as an amplifier for the information received. It is important to note that all dowsing is affected by the subconscious beliefs of the dowser.

Anyone can learn to dowse, because dowsing taps resources available to all. There are many kinds of dowsing, but to explore your strands, start with a pendulum, because it is one of the easier methods to master. (To use dowsing to cut cords, see the exercise on page 107 in Chapter 3.)

Here are the steps to follow to begin dowsing:

Create or obtain a pendulum. If you do decide to purchase a pendulum, find one that both looks and feels good to you. Try it out before you buy it. Pendulums can be made from stones, crystals, lead crystals, wood, or metal, and they can be very beautiful. The best pendulums are symmetrical in shape with a point at one end, but other shapes will also work.

Before you begin to work with your pendulum, you will want to energize it. You can do this by holding your hands over it and imagining that light is radiating out of your hands into the pendulum. Energizing your pendulum will almost always improve the way it works for you.

The next step is to hold the cord or chain firmly between your thumb and index finger, several inches from the pendulum (a comfortable range is between 3 and 12 inches) so that it can swing freely and smoothly. Pressing your elbow firmly against your body or placing it on a table will help steady you and ground your energy.

Learn how your pendulum provides answers. To get accustomed to using the pendulum, ask it a question to which you already know the answer. This will help you decipher movements, which indicate yes or no to further questions. For example, if you ask your pendulum, "Does the earth revolve around the sun?" and it swings in a direction perpendicular to your body in response, then you will know that this movement indicates yes for your particular pendulum. Usually, although not always, when the pendulum swings perpendicular to the front of your body it means yes, while a swing parallel to your body means no.

Clockwise swinging usually means yes, and counterclockwise usually means no.

To familiarize yourself with your pendulum, it is good to practice by asking very simple, straightforward questions, such as "Am I male?" or "Is it daytime?" When it's clear which movement indicates yes and which indicates no, you can ask your pendulum questions about other things you would like to know. However, before seeking information from your pendulum, you should always ask the following questions of yourself:

- *Can I?* This question relates to whether or not you have the prerequisite knowledge for receiving the answer you seek. For example, if you are asking about idea strands but you don't really know what an idea strand is, then the pendulum will be of limited use to you in dowsing for it.

- *Should I?* This question asks you to consider carefully whether or not it would be in your best interest to receive knowledge about this issue at this particular time. It also asks you to consider if it would be helpful for everyone concerned. Sometimes we are not ready to receive the answers to our questions.

If your answer is yes to both of the above questions, then you are ready to go ahead and use your pendulum for dowsing. Remember to ask simple, clear questions. Experienced dowsers have mastered the skill of asking questions in a concise manner. The way you frame your question will determine how useful the information you receive will be.

Once you have begun, don't worry if the pendulum doesn't respond immediately. Sometimes beginners become so afraid of getting a wrong answer that they freeze up. Consciously release the idea that you need to be right. Completely clear your mind. When your own thoughts are quiet, you will function as an antenna, accessing your own subconscious and the collective unconscious. Dowsing is not a force that can be controlled. You are a channel. Sometimes answers will flow easily through you; sometimes nothing will come at all. Let go. When you are relaxed and enjoy-ing yourself, you will be able to achieve much better results. And, as with most skills, you will get better with practice.

In the case of an unmoving pendulum, it sometimes helps to hold it in your hands for several minutes, or rub it in one direc-tion, or breathe on it. These techniques often increase the respon-siveness of a pendulum.

Trust your first reaction. When you have practiced with questions to which you know the answers, progress to ones you don't know the answers to but can find out. The most important thing is to trust whatever is revealed to you. It's all right to be discerning with the information, but please don't constantly doubt yourself. When asking a new question, stop the pendulum completely and start again. The more practice you have, the more accurate you will become and the more your confidence will increase. Once you have gained confidence about your dowsing abilities, you can begin to apply this skill to exploring your strands.

After you are comfortable with your pendulum, you can begin asking about different people and different situations to see where your biggest affinity strands are. You may be surprised. Usually your first response is best.

My suggestion is to use yes and no questions. For example, you might ask, "Do I have a strong cord to Charlene?" If you get a yes, then a second question might be, "Is this a positive connection?" And you can continue onward; each question gives more informa-tion. Remember, each time before you ask a new question, reset the pendulum. You may want to write down the information you are receiving.

Recognize degrees of truth. Sometimes an answer isn't either yes or no, but rather is expressed in terms of degrees, or percentages, of rightness. For example, if you are dowsing about how much effect a strand from your Aunt Gail has on your energy, you might find that particular strand has a 48 percent effect on you, while your friend Susan has an 8 percent effect on you. You can also dowse to see negative and positive impacts on your energy field. You can use the shading of the graph to determine this. If the pendulum goes into the darkest areas of your chart, you might see that that particular strand has a debilitating effect on you; if it swings into a lightly shaded area, you can see that it has a minimal effect on you.

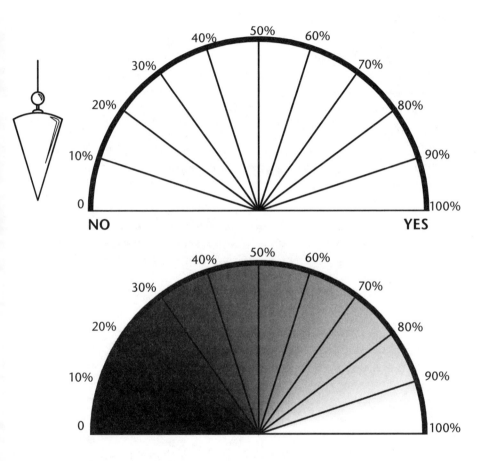

Discover the energy drains in your home. Some of the biggest drains to our energy can be the cords that attach us to our home and to the objects in it. (This is why clutter clearing can have such a powerful impact on your energy.) You can use your pendulum while walking through your home or living environment to see if you have any strands to particular areas or objects that are weakening you. Simply stand in different areas or focus on different objects and notice if the pendulum is indicating a yes, meaning that it is a good energy connection, or a no, which can indicate a negative attachment. You can use this information to clear out objects with which you have negative cord attachments. (For example, if the silver tea set that your grandmother gave you reminds you of how manipulative she was, there might be negative strands attaching it to you.)

You can also scan your living environment within a meditative state. Here's how: Relax. Close your eyes and imagine that you are slowly walking through your home, room by room. In each room, stop and tune in to the energy there. Imagine that you have the ability to perceive energy, and notice what cords attach to particular objects and particular areas. Notice if your energy goes up or down with each object.

In this chapter, you've learned the effects of negative strands, how to explore and assess them, and when it's a good idea to think about releasing them. In the next chapter, you'll learn exact methods to sever links that are depleting you.

CHAPTER THREE

CUTTING THE TIES THAT BIND: RELEASING THE STRANDS THAT DIMINISH YOU

This chapter is for the times when you need to unhook or let go of someone or something from your life. You'll learn how to release, sever, or diminish cords that are depleting you. However, it's important to remember that when your energy is strong and clear and your frequency is attuned, negative cords shrink without you doing anything. Before we jump into cutting and releasing strands and cords, there are some things to keep in mind.

Randomly cutting strands, without a clear intention of why you are doing it—and without understanding the underlying reasons for those strands—can sometimes cause an imbalance in your energy. You need to have a conscious awareness of *why* you want to sever a connection and also have a respect for the sacred process of releasing a strand.

It's valuable to remember that on some level, you have chosen the attachment of the strands of energy that you have . . . even the ones that aren't healthy. Of course, most likely it wasn't a conscious decision to have those negative cords, but from a spiritual perspective, you may have "signed up" or have a "life contract" for those strands to attach to you. (A life contract consists of choices that you made about your current life, pre-birth, while you were in the spirit world, usually with the intent to grow spiritually as a result.) On a very deep level, there is always personal—albeit usually unconscious—responsibility for every life experience.

It's not enjoyable to think that we get something out of the depleting energy attachments that we have, but perhaps we are victims of life because of the way our society honors and even celebrates victims. Television news is full of victim stories, and we all rush to pity and feel sorry for those for who have life tragedies. In our culture, it's often easier to feel like a victim than to acknowledge responsibility for our life experiences. Of course, we should have immense compassion for anyone in trying circumstances. We should also have compassion for ourselves if we have a rough time in life. But it's important to remember that from a *spiritual* perspective, there are no victims, only volunteers.

IS THERE A PAYOFF FOR HAVING NEGATIVE STRANDS?

Here are some hard questions to answer, but they are helpful for you in your journey to understanding and releasing strands that don't serve you. Please don't judge yourself if you answer yes to any of these questions. It just means that you are human. Almost all of us, if we are being honest, will answer in the affirmative to one or more of these questions.

- Do you subconsciously enjoy the feeling of being needed, even if needy people are depleting some of your energy? Do you need to be needed?

- Have you given your power away to someone in an effort for that person to like you?

- Has your need for approval ever overridden the needs of your soul?

- Do you have a dysfunctional relationship with yourself that causes you to tend to draw negative relationships into your life?

- Do you enjoy getting to be right about a person or situation you don't like?

- Do you get to add drama to your life by declaring to others something like, "Jane is an energy vampire!"?

- Do you find yourself being a bit righteous about a belief you hold or an organization you belong to?

- Do you like feeling that you are a "good guy" and *they* are the "bad guys"?

- Do you enjoy constantly rushing out to be the "hero," and thus attract toxic cords and situations into your life so that you can right the wrongs?

- Do you create an overabundance of strand attachments because you equate busyness with your personal value?

- Do you have flimsy personal boundaries and suffer from the need to please?

- Do you find yourself reworking a conversation you had with someone again and again, wishing you had said something else and feeling guilty for what you did say? Or do you resent that person for not being the kind of person you could say anything to, without being worried about how they would take it?

- Do you easily take offense when it seems someone has judged you and then feel righteous about your response?

If you answer yes to any of these questions, they might indicate a kind of payoff for having attachments in your life. For example, the instant you take offense about what someone said to you or did to you, a cord gets attached. The payoff is that you get to be righteous. If you observe that they were inappropriate, but you don't have an emotional gut response, there is no strand. It's hard to look at ourselves with stark self-scrutiny and realize that, in some cases, there *is* something we get out of the negative energy attachments that we have, even the ones we detest. This kind of self-examination is the first step to releasing negative strands.

WHAT ARE THE ROOTS OF YOUR STRANDS?

It's valuable to explore the roots of the attachments you have before you begin cutting. To truly be free, you need to heal and resolve underlying issues that have precipitated the attachments. If you don't do this, cutting an energy cord can sometimes be a short-term solution. The energy strands will reestablish themselves if you don't understand and heal why they are there in the first place. If you cut cords but don't address the underlying reasons that you have them, they may keep coming back.

Sometimes negative strand attachments can represent something in yourself that you aren't owning or acknowledging. It's not uncommon to have an energy strand connection to someone who has qualities that you haven't activated in yourself. For example, a woman might have a cord attachment to someone on the national scene in politics who has tremendous confidence because she subconsciously yearns to activate her own self-esteem. She hasn't owned it yet, so she cord-attaches to someone who has it. That particular strand can represent a lack of personal power on her part.

Here's another example. Gerald carries a lot of suppressed anger; he believes he is a peaceful person, but anyone around him can attest to the seething emotions that Gerald has just beneath the surface. Most of his co-workers have labeled him as passive-aggressive. Because he hasn't accepted his own anger, whenever

Gerald encounters anyone who is angry, he harshly judges them. He hasn't owned his own anger, so he projects his criticism of himself onto others with the same condition. Gerald thus thrusts a strand of energy into each person he disapproves of. As long as he judges himself, he can't help it. In other words, he becomes hooked into and corded to the energetic fields of a number of angry people. Consequently, his energy centers are clogged with anger—both his and others.

Understanding the source of your negative strands is immensely valuable. The great thing is that, as you unweave your own issues, the people who were attracted or corded to the dysfunctional parts of you will start dropping away.

THEY ARE NOT DEMON SPAWN (NECESSARILY)

Please don't make the mistake of feeling that the person you want to cut away is a monster and you are an innocent victim. This kind of strong judgment creates all kinds of energy strands of its own and can gum up the works in your auric field. (Remember: they wouldn't be able to cord to you if there wasn't anything to attach to.)

I know there are times when it can feel like they really are demon spawn. I also know—from personal experience—that it can be very difficult to let go of angst when you are around someone who is cruel, unfair, or unkind. However, in the end, this kind of emotion can damage you and also makes it almost impossible to clear their energy out of your energy field.

If you have been truly wronged by another, *the best revenge is to clear them completely out of your energy field forever.* And to do this, you need to let go. You need to surrender your judgment and the need to be right about them. It's one of the most difficult things a human being can do, yet it brings great rewards. You will feel lighter and more at peace with yourself and with the world.

It's important to know that cutting cords won't necessarily change someone; if they were a jerk before, they will probably be a jerk afterward. Cutting the cord just means that they aren't entangled in your energy, and thus they aren't creating problems for you.

Sometimes the person with whom you have cut the cord will suddenly call you, right after you release the connection, wanting to reconnect. On an energetic level, they felt the disconnection and want to reel you back in to their life. If this is a past dysfunctional relationship, this call doesn't necessarily mean they want you back in their life; it might mean they want to continue to pull energy from you or even control you. If a person you have just released tries to get back into your life, it's best to simply wish them love and ignore their calls.

SOMETIMES YOU DON'T NEED TO CUT A CORD

Before you diminish any cords, see if there is something you can do physically to stop the depletion of your energy. Sometimes you don't actually have to cut the cords; just simply shifting a few things can make a huge difference. For example, if there is a relative that you constantly feel drained around, sometimes simply spending less time with them can help weaken the cord connection. Or if you have strand attachments to objects in your home that have negative associations, some clutter clearing can move them out of your energy field.

It may seem simpler just to do a strand cutting ceremony; however, some objects in your home have such strong associations that the cords may form again. Sometimes it's better to simply move the object out of your home and your life. You can do this with relationships as well; spend less time with people who diminish your energy, and you may not need to do any cord clearing.

BECOME CENTERED AND FOCUSED
BEFORE ANY CUTTING

Before any cord cutting, it's valuable to be able to hone your energy. This will make your ceremony more powerful. To do this, begin by entering into a meditative state. If your mind begins to wander, gently but firmly bring it back. It helps to have a visual image to focus on, or a mantra to say, in order to keep your mind focused. For example, you might imagine a rose. Visualize every soft curve of its petals. Imagine its fragrance. Notice where the stem attaches to the flower. Be so attuned to the rose that everything else just drops away. When you can maintain this discipline for 20 minutes of a calm, dedicated, meditative state, then you can be successful at releasing the cords that bind you.

Some of these cord-cutting methods incorporate visualization. Don't be concerned if you aren't able to visualize immediately. It is your *intent* that creates results. Hold a clear, focused intent, and you'll be able to clear cords just as effectively as if you were visualizing.

Sometimes people tell me that they think cutting cords or shielding can't really work if it's just visualization. Actually, visualization can be one of the most powerful methods. When my daughter, Meadow, was about three and a half years old, an acquaintance named Ruth had come into our home, and I could feel my energy tanking as we talked. To stop the energy depletion, I visualized a beautiful pink rose between Ruth and me. I wanted to mitigate the disturbing energy that was flowing between us, and it made a huge difference. Instantly, my energy started to recover. Just at that time, Meadow toddled out into the living room, pointed at the space between Ruth and me, and said, "Mommy, Mommy! Look at the rose! Pretty!" She "saw" the rose that I had visualized. It was a powerful affirmation of the potency of visualization. Your visualization indeed has weight and measure.

As a note, just because you release cords with someone doesn't mean that you can't have a wonderful relationship with them. Often it improves a relationship. It doesn't mean that you don't care or that you don't want to be friends with that person. It just means that any damaging or depleting cords are dissolved. It frees you to have more energy and vitality. It also allows you to set clear boundaries. Your emotions will be *your* emotions. Your thoughts will be *your* thoughts. The opposite of fear is love, and dysfunctional strands usually come out of fear. Release the fear, step into love, and any negative cords will just drop away.

CORD-CLEARING METHODS

In this chapter, I share a number of potent methods to release cords and strands that aren't healthy for you. Which method should you use? They all work. Some work better for one person than another. My suggestion is to try a few, and soon you'll discover the ones that are most effective for you.

Clearing Method 1: Cutting Strands with Knives— Physical and Nonphysical

Whether you do this method in a physical or nonphysical way, it needs to be done with compassion and a powerful intent. If you are upset or angry while you do it, you might be able to cut the cord, but your anger will cleave the person's energy toward you and the cord will reattach. I know this isn't easy. Obviously, if you are cutting a cord, it's because it is causing imbalances in your life. Or it's because you are distressed by someone. However, the more you can detach and become the "sacred observer" with the understanding that there was a reason for attachment—and on some level, you gained value from it—the easier it will be to dismantle it.

Nonphysical Cord Cutting

1. **Cleanse yourself.** Take a shower, scrub with salt, and then have a cold rinse. (This refreshes your auric field.) You can also take a saltwater bath, with a cold rinse. Wear light-colored clean

clothes. (Light colors reflect and dark colors absorb; you want the unhealthy attachment deflected, rather than absorbed.)

2. Drink plenty of water. It's important to be hydrated for this type of ceremony. Energized water is best. To energize water, either hold your hand over it and bless it, or leave it out in the sun (or under the moon and stars) for at least five hours with the intent of the heavenly forces energizing it.

3. Write it down. Be clear on exactly who and/or what you will release. Sometimes it helps to write down exactly what you desire and place it on your personal altar. If you don't have an altar, light a candle and place the list under the candle.

4. Sit in a comfortable location. Close your eyes and relax. It's worthwhile to have some ambient music in the background. Music can allow you to go deeper faster. Take a few very deep, full breaths. With each inhalation, imagine that shimmering, fresh energy is filling you, and all that is not needed is being released with every exhalation.

5. Call upon guides. Call upon your spiritual guides, angels, and ancestors to offer support and guidance. Ask, with gratitude, that they help you release what is not needed, for the highest good of all.

6. Visualize. Once you feel relaxed, imagine that you are atop a high grassy hill. In the far distance, you might see snowcapped mountains or a luminous seashore. Spend time getting a sense of this lofty vantage point. Imagine that the high grasses are slowly waving in a gentle breeze. See white fluffy clouds overhead. Take a moment to feel strong and grounded. There is a meandering pathway that leads to the top of the hill. Anyone or anything that has attachments to you can come up the pathway to you, as you desire.

7. Cut and release. You notice that in your hands you have large sharp shears, scissors, or a knife. It feels holy. As the first person you desire to cut cords with appears on the path, imagine that they are standing in front of you. Look at the strands that connect you. If they are brightly colored and vibrant, you may consider leaving them. If you see any that look dark and dull or shriveled, take your shears (or scissors or knife) and cut that cord. If your knife begins to feel dull, hold it above your head to be sharpened by the light of the sun. Sometimes you'll cut a cord and it seems to come back. Just keep cutting again and again, or even pull it out. Eventually it will stay severed.

8. Affirm. As you cut, with a clear intent say, "What is mine is mine. What is yours is yours." Or you can say:

- "I, (state your name), hereby release and sever all cords to you that do not serve and support our highest good."

- "As I cut the ties to you, I honor my space . . . and I honor your space. We each stand free in our own light. I am free. You are free."

- "Only that which is beneficial and empowering remains."

When you make your verbal declaration, you should feel an immediate lightening of your energy field.

9. Offer gratitude. Thank the person (or object or situation) for being in your life, then send them sincere blessings for their own journey. This is an important part of the process. It completes the cycle and makes it easier for you to go forward in your life without the attachment.

Physical Cord Cutting

Physical cord cutting combines visualization with the use of a real knife, shears, or scissors. The steps are similar to the previous method; however, instead of sitting, stand strong. Hold the tool that you are going to use for the severing. Instead of visualizing the knife (or other tool) severing the cords, actually take the knife and cut or slice through the air where you perceive the cord to be. Pay particular attention to the solar plexus area, as this is the area most often clogged by attachments. *Be careful not to cut yourself.* Always keep your eyes open when cutting. Make sure that the instrument you use is later washed and then rinsed in very cold water to cleanse it of residual energies.

Black String Method

Use this method in a ceremonial way. Obtain a photo of the person from whom you want to cut strands and a photo of yourself. Roll each photo into an individual scroll, and wrap a black string, black cord, or black yarn around one. (If you don't have photos, simply write your names on pieces of paper, and make them into your scrolls.) Then, leaving at least nine inches of thread or string between the two scrolls, wrap the second scroll with the remaining string. In a meditative space, hold the intent that all that is not needed is released. You might say or pray:

> I INVOKE THE PURE LIGHT OF SPIRIT
> TO FLOW THROUGH ME.
> I AM EMBRACED AND PROTECTED
> BY THE LOVE OF THE CREATOR.
> ONLY THAT WHICH SUPPORTS AND
> NURTURES ME IS ATTACHED TO ME.
> I AM SAFE, STRONG, AND WELL. ALL IS WELL.

Then, take your scissors or knife and cut the cord cleanly. I suggest taking the two parts and disposing of them at a distance apart, such as burying them or, ideally, burning them with the intent that all cords are clear and bright and in accordance with the highest good.

Traditional Knife Use for Cutting Cords

Using a knife to cut cords is very traditional. I was at a wedding in Bali and the person officiating had an ornate Balinese knife that was used to symbolically cut any cords to others, so as to cleave the couple together.

In Tibet, a knife called a *kartika* is a decorated, crescent-shaped knife that is used to cut or sever material and worldly bonds that do not serve you. The knife is decorated with a *varja* on top, which is a bulblike decoration that is thought to help destroy ignorance, which in turn leads to enlightenment. Another kind of knife used in Tibetan Buddhism is the *phurba*. This is a three-sided ceremonial knife that has many uses; however, one of the ways Tibetans use it is to dispel "demon thought forms" and then administer purification. It's believed that the *phurba* can cut negative ties to entities, people, and thought forms, including those generated by a group. Thought forms are energy manifestations of the thoughts, ideas, or emotions of an individual or of a group of people. Some people can sense them, such as when they enter into a space after an argument has taken place; they can feel the heaviness in the room.

Other traditions also use a ceremonial knife for cutting ties. In neo-pagan traditions, a knife called an *athame* is used to direct energy (but not to cut cords) and a knife called a *boline,* which is curved and looks like a sickle, is used to cut negative energy cords, among other things.

I've been told that in some Native American traditions, a bear claw or an eagle talon is used to symbolically pull out cords; although this feels accurate, I don't have research that supports this.

Using a Crystal or a Stone for Physical Cord Cutting

The steps for using a crystal or a stone for physical cord cutting are similar to the above methods; however, make sure that you use a faceted or terminated crystal or stone rather than a tumbled one. Black obsidian that has been chipped into an arrowhead or a knife is a powerful tool for cord cutting. A black tourmaline wand is also excellent. Use these objects the same way that you would use a knife.

Clearing Method 2: Wrap, Pull, and Ground

This method is best done outdoors, but it can also be done as an inner meditative journey. This method is like pulling a weed out of the earth by its roots.

Outdoors: Wrap, Pull, and Ground

1. Barefoot and centered. If you are doing this method outdoors, it's best to be barefoot upon the earth, preferably near a tree. Placing your weight equally on both legs, gently rock back and forth and side to side until you feel that you have found your center point. Be still and imagine that you are a tree of life, and your roots are reaching deep into the earth and your branches are soaring high into the sky.

2. Observing. With your eyes closed, imagine that you are scanning your body. Notice any cords that are coarse or dull. It's not necessary to follow every strand to its source. Simply being aware of a strand, thread, or filament that isn't vibrating with life-force energy is enough.

3. Wrapping. Locate the first strand you desire to remove and imagine you are wrapping your hand around it to secure it. (You can do this physically with your hand or visualize yourself doing it.)

4. Pulling. Once the strand feels secure, with a gentle but steady pressure, pull it out. You might need to gently wiggle it back and forth to get it to release. It can feel like gently pulling a weed out by its roots so that it comes out whole and doesn't break off. Sometimes you may feel a physical sensation inside your body as this happens. This is not uncommon, and it is nothing to be concerned about. You will know when the strand is removed; there will no longer be any tension on it.

5. Grounding. Once the cord is removed, quickly reach down and place the end of it on the earth to ground and neutralize it. Mother

Earth can transmute all energy attachments. Then imagine all the holes left by the cord in your body filling with light and love.

You can repeat this process with every negative strand you discover. When you are finished, take a long shower and make sure that you have a cold rinse. Alternatively, take an Epsom-salt bath and end with a cold rinse. Within 24 hours, you should notice a substantial difference.

Indoors: Wrap, Pull, and Ground

This same method can be done indoors as a visualization, and it can be just as effective; it's just a matter of having a very clear intention as you do it. Make sure you cleanse yourself afterward in a similar way as well.

Clearing Method 3: Spirit Pruning

Another powerful method of clearing depleting ties is to ask for spirit support. This support can be from your guides, totems, ancestors, angels, or the Creator. Call for their support; it can feel like a kind of "spirit pruning," where your higher guides are trimming what isn't needed from your soul. For example, call upon Archangel Michael. *His support is one of the most powerful ways to clear cords!* Ask that his flaming sword of light cleave anything that is not needed by saying:

Archangel Michael, with deep gratitude I invoke thee to assist me and (the other person's name) to release any limiting ties that bind us to each other. I acknowledge my part in this attachment and honor the lessons that I have learned. I am now ready to release and let go.

I ask that all cords be dissolved and transmuted for the highest good for us both. I request forgiveness and peace to flow between us and to seal us each in our individual spheres of energy with love.

Alternatively, you can visualize one of your spirit guides removing energy threads that are depleting you. You might actually see them using their sacred shears and pruning them the same way you might prune an overgrown tree. You can imagine that you are in a temple or a hallowed place while the cords are pruned. Remember the very important step of being grateful for all that is released. This deepens the results that you gain.

Clearing Method 4: Dowsing and Dissolving

As we learned in Chapter 2, the pendulum is a potent tool to help you understand what cords are attached to you. It can also be used for releasing energy attachments. Here are the steps:

1. Imagine the ropes or strands. Visualize that the cords you want to cut are in front of you; imagine them between you and the person, addictive behavior, object, or belief that you desire to sever.

2. Hold the pendulum up in front of you. As you hold the pendulum in front of you, allow it to spin or swing back and forth. In the beginning, it may feel that *you* are doing it. That's okay. There may come a time when it feels that it is moving on its own, but until that time, it's okay to feel that you are controlling it.

3. Visualize vibrant light radiating out from the pendulum. Imagine that as the pendulum swings or spirals, the light is getting brighter and brighter. This swinging or spiraling light is severing any cords that are not needed.

4. Start above your head. While the pendulum is moving (much like the way a clock pendulum swings), hold it a few inches in front of you, or take it above your head. Slowly lower the pendulum. As it gradually goes lower and lower in front of your body, it is cutting cords. (If it feels right, you could alternatively start at your pubic bone area and bring the swinging pendulum up your body.)

5. Let it stop on its own. Don't be concerned about how fast or slow your pendulum spins or swings. Allow it to travel at its own speed. Sometimes it will feel as if it has a mind of its own. This is a good thing. Let it stop on its own; allow it to complete the process that has begun. When this occurs, the cords have been cut.

Clearing Method 5: Violet Flame, Golden Light

This is my favorite method. I love it because it works in such an easy, flowing way. I also love it because I don't need to figure out what I am cutting away; the transmuting energy of the flame cleanses only what isn't needed.

The first time I encountered the power of the violet flame was decades ago. I had been in a back room of our home and walked into the living room . . . and stopped abruptly. It felt completely different. My ordinary living room seemed alive. It looked and felt so vibrant and sparkling. I asked my friend Lynette, who was visiting from South Africa at the time, "What happened in the living room?!"

She shyly answered that she had done a violet flame clearing of the room. "I hope that was okay," she murmured.

"It's more than okay! It's fabulous! The radiant feeling in the room is palpable. I want to learn how to do that!"

Lynette explained that the violet flame transmutes negative into positive energy, releases cords attachments, clears karma, raises one's frequency, accelerates spiritual growth, and can even offer a shield of protection. The violet color has the highest frequency on the visible color spectrum. (If you look closely at a rainbow, at the far edge of the rainbow, you'll see a tiny bit of this color.) It's a color that many spiritual adepts utilize in their meditations for clearing.

Since that time, I have used the violet flame with powerful results. Simply visualizing this color as a flame, with very focused intention, can activate its cleansing qualities. Here are some steps to use this powerful method for releasing unhealthy strands of energy.

You might consider playing Schubert's "Ave Maria" while you do the method below, as it can help activate the violet flame.

Violet Flame to Melt Cords

1. Cleanse. Take a refreshing shower, making sure to scrub all over, and end with a cold rinse, or take a salt bath and end with a cold rinse. Wear clean, light-colored clothing.

2. Light a candle. The instant the match flame touches the wick of the candle can be a hallowed moment. In that moment, focus a deliberate intention on clearing your strands.

3. Relax. Take a few very deep breaths, and allow your body to move into a relaxed state.

4. Place your awareness in your heart chakra. Imagine that in the center of your chest there is a tiny violet flame. (Some people like to start in the third-eye area, which works equally well.) Concentrate on the flame as it becomes bigger and bigger and brighter and brighter. See it pulsating, undulating, and shimmering until your entire body is encased in it.

5. Affirm out loud. Call upon the higher energies of the violet flame to blaze through you, and affirm, "I am one with the violet flame. The violet flame flows through me and exists within me. All that is not needed is dissolving and transmuting into higher frequencies. So be it, and so it is."

6. Completion. You can tell when the process is complete because when you tune in, the sparking, crackling, and wild undulating of the flame slows down and it becomes more like a single flame in the center of a still monastery than a blaze in a wind gust.

Golden Light to Melt Cords

Here is another clearing method that I love. This meditation is similar to the violet flame, but it works with the golden light and also with communication . . . higher self to higher self. The first three steps—cleanse, light a candle, and relax into a meditative state—are the same as the violet flame method. Here are the next steps:

4. Connect with the higher self. In your meditation, imagine the higher self of the person you desire to detach from. See the person as perfect. Even if it is a challenge, visualize the person in their natural state, without fear, anger, resentment, control issues, and/or manipulative behavior. Imagine that individual healthy, whole, and filled with light. If you have difficulty doing this, imagine what they might have been like if their life circumstances had been different. Remember, almost all bad behavior comes from fear, and if they had different life experiences, different past lives, and a different upbringing, they might be balanced, gracious, and kind, rather than acting out of fear or ignorance. You can also imagine that individual as an innocent, joyous child, if this makes it easier to see them in a positive light.

5. Share and listen. Imagine that their higher self is standing before you. Tell this individual how you feel about the relationship and how you feel you have suffered because of what has occurred between you. Speak honestly and from your heart. *Then take time to listen to what their higher self has to say.* Sometimes there is an apology, sometimes there is an explanation, and sometimes there is a sharing of hurt and pain. Allow them the opportunity to share openly and freely. Listen with an open heart, without trying to defend yourself or tell them why they are wrong. Simply listen.

6. Forgiveness. It is not necessary to forgive someone's actions—some actions are unforgiveable—but it is possible to forgive the person. Ask yourself if you are willing to forgive that individual who is standing before you. (Remember, you can forgive without condoning their actions.) It is much easier to release the cords if you can forgive. If you can't pardon them, and you continue to be filled with resentment, bitterness, or anger, the cords cling to you. If you just can't quite forgive them, then forgive yourself for *not* forgiving. It's an excellent first step.

7. Observe the strands. Look at the space between you and the other. Notice what strands connect you. Do some look healthy and some dim and dull? (As mentioned before, it's possible to relinquish the unhealthy ones and keep the vibrant ones, if you desire.)

8. Invoke the golden light. Invoke or put out the call for the golden light to come forth:

I CALL UPON THE GOLDEN LIGHT
OF SPIRIT TO COME FORTH.
WITH GRATITUDE, I ASK THAT THIS LIGHT
DISMISS ALL THAT IS NOT NEEDED, AND PURIFY
AND PROTECT ME IN THE MONTHS TO COME.
BLESSINGS. BLESSINGS. BLESSINGS.

Imagine that between your hands is a ball of golden glowing light that grows in vibrancy and warmth. This is the light of the Divinity. Hold this light over your head and then slowly bring it down over your body. You might notice golden light streaming out of your hands too. Pay particular attention to the areas of your chakras. Notice as this light flows over the strands how it melts and dissolves unhealthy ones and how it purifies and strengthens healthy ones. Your entire body is radiating and pulsating with resplendent light. This intense, all-pervasive light is healing you, protecting you, and dissolving all that is not needed. Then take the ball up your body, bringing grounding earth energy into your auric field, and lift the ball up to the heavens, letting it float upward and away.

6. Offer gratitude. Offer gratitude and blessings for all that was given. Gratitude helps seal the de-cording and makes it difficult for new cords to attach.

Clearing Method 6: Clearing Cords with Feathers

Since the beginning of human history, feathers have been a favored tool of shamans and native people for ceremonies and rituals. In many tribal traditions, birds are thought to be the messengers between the spirit realm and the physical; thus, their feathers are venerated as the conduit between these two worlds. Because the quill of the feather is an open tube, many cultures believe it serves as a channel for prayers and energy. It's considered to be a pathway of communication with spirit messengers or supernatural beings.

In indigenous cultures, feathers are used for a variety of purposes. For example, there are feathers for healing, dancing, success in hunting and fishing, clearing and protecting a home, and bringing rain, among many others. There are friendship feathers (to give to your mentors, friends, or those whom you respect), answering feathers (to hold to receive an answer to your questions), and smudging feathers (for space clearing). Feathers are also bestowed in recognition of a brave act or a worthy accomplishment. They can also be used to sever or clear strands.

Because of their delicate attunement to the finer aspects of energy, feathers are useful for all phases of energy clearing, from the initial assessment to the cutting of cords. The feather can allow you to tune in to levels of awareness that may have previously been inaccessible to you. If your intention is clearly focused, a single feather can instantly sever any unbeneficial strands.

When using a feather to clear your own energy and shear off cords of negative energy that are attached to you, you will want to begin by taking the time to deeply connect with the energy of the feather. Hold it next to your heart and imagine yourself merging with the energy of the feather and the spirit of the individual bird from which it came. As you become one with the spirit of the bird, together you will work to achieve the magic of the strand release.

Begin with short flicking movements, working from head to toe over the entire body. Imagine that your feather has the cutting ability of a very sharp etheric knife. If you come to a place that seems to feel sticky or somehow heavy, this can indicate that the energy is stuck or stagnant there. Concentrate your efforts with the feather in this area, making short, quick cutting movements to break up the energy before you move on.

Once you feel the energy beginning to change and you sense a cord has been cut, switch to long, smooth strokes of the feather to even out the energy. Long, graceful movements can smooth out and calm erratic energy after cords have been cut. Always be sure to cleanse your feathers after using them for cord cutting. Passing them through the smoke of burning sage, cedar, or juniper can do this.

Choosing your feather. Every feather has an individual energy. The best feathers are the ones that choose you. These are the ones that appear seemingly out of nowhere. Additionally, a feather that is gifted to you from a person who honors the Native American medicine way also has great potency. Of course, you can also purchase your feather. Usually stores that supply fly-tying equipment for fisherman and craft stores have a supply of feathers. Also, vendors at powwows often carry feathers and feather fans for sale. However, don't just grab one and say, "This will do." To find the best feather for you at a shop or booth, become very relaxed and let your eyelids lower slightly, then put out the call or ask that your feather appear to you. Often you'll see a feather that seems more radiant than the other ones. This is a sign that it's meant for you.

Caring for your feather. Treating your feathers with the respect they deserve enhances their effectiveness. You will want to keep them in a special place and "feed" them by occasionally sprinkling them with a bit of cornmeal and then shaking it off. Doing so symbolically feeds the spirit of the bird and replenishes the feather's energy.

Many birds have mites that may be present in feathers. If feathers are left untreated, these mites will eventually eat your feathers away and destroy their beauty and usefulness. Storing your feathers in cedar, sage, borax, or tobacco can help prevent this type of degradation.

Forms of feathers to use in cord cutting. Feathers used for cord cutting come in three traditional forms: single feathers, feather fans, and wings. You can use a single unadorned feather, or you can decorate it by wrapping the end of the quill with leather or cloth. This leather or cloth, in turn, can be decorated with more strips of leather and beads.

Another option is to use a feather fan, which is usually made from several feathers gathered together and secured with a piece of leather or a wooden base. Wings and feather fans have a wider surface for moving energy but are a little less easy to control than a single feather.

Clearing Method 7: Smudging

A delicate plume of smoke curling upward through still air evokes immediate and powerful associations with ritual, purification, and spiritual connections. For thousands of years, humans everywhere have burned herbs, scented wood, resins, and other aromatic substances as a way to channel their hopes, prayers, and dreams to the realm of spirit, as well as to purify living spaces and each other.

Smoke purifies and transports. It transforms the ordinary into the sacred. It speaks directly to one of our most powerful and primordial senses, the sense of smell, a sense integrally connected to buried memories, emotions, and perception. Because of this connection, the use of smoke can powerfully and instantly change energy. It's also believed that our prayers can travel on plumes of smoke and blessings from the Creator can descend down the plumes as well.

In shamanic traditions, burning herbs are used to clear negative energy from people and places. This practice is called "smudging." When I spent time with the Zulu in Africa, they used burning herbs to cleanse the energy of anyone who had been released from prison or returned from war. They believe that the energy of those dark places clings to someone when they return home and could affect family members. In other words, there were still lingering cords from those places and from the experiences they had there. Hence, the Zulu would use burning herbs to cleanse and release the cords.

In most of the other native cultures that I've spent time in, the smoke of special burning herbs is also believed to release cords and clear negative energy. When I was in Brazil talking with a shaman there, he said they used burning herbs to clear negative energy from places. He said they would fill a place with so much smoke you could hardly see, and then they would open a window to release all the "bad" energy.

Sage and cedar for smudging. One of the most potent herbs used for clearing energy is sage. Traditionally used by the Plains Indians, sage has gained great popularity in recent years because of its very powerful and potent ability to cleanse and purify people and spaces. Its effects are instantly noticeable, so it is a good choice to release negative cords of energy. The pungent smell of sage smoke is excellent for dispelling particularly heavy or stagnant energy and releasing dark, sticky cords. The Cherokees (my tribe), as well as a number of other tribes, traditionally used cedar for the same purpose. Different kinds of herbs are used in different countries, but the type of herb used is less important than the intent and prayer that is used with it.

"Washing" Your Auric Field with Smoke

Here is a method to cleanse your auric field with smoke and release strands of challenging energy.

1. Place a bowl of smoking herbs or incense on a table or counter, and then draw the smoke to your body with your cupped hands.

2. Wash the smoke over your head with the words, "That my thoughts may be pure."

3. Then wash the smoke over your eyes, saying, "That I may see the truth."

4. Wash the smoke over your ears, saying, "That I may hear the truth."

5. Then wash the smoke over your throat, saying, "That I may speak the truth."

6. Wash the smoke over your heart, saying, "That my heart may be open and clear."

7. Wash the smoke down your entire body saying, "That my body may be strong."

8. Draw the smoke to each of your chakras, with the intention of releasing unneeded cords.

As you draw the smoke over your body, focus your thoughts on your intention for the clearing. Know that the smoke is cleansing you of distractions and negativity. It is purifying your mind and body in readiness for the energy work that you are about to do. This is an excellent method to use for purifying your aura before performing a cutting ceremony. It also can help remove smaller attachments, such as filament and thread strands.

Smudge bundles. A smudging bundle is created of dried herbs bunched together and then wrapped tightly with string; this is traditionally burned to create smoke for smudging. The dried smudge bundle is first lit and then extinguished, allowing the still smoldering herbs to give off their pungent smoke. (Please note cautions below concerning the use of burning herbs.) These bundles are one of the easiest and most common ways to use herbs for smudging. You can make your own herb bundles or buy them at a New Age store or via mail order. Sage is probably the most common herb used for smudging, but other herbs work equally well.

The smoke of a smudge bundle instantly creates an enormous shift in energy. It's also one of the best methods to use when you need to shift your entire energy field. To smudge your body with the intention of releasing cord attachments, place the burning herbs in a container filled with sand (to keep the container from getting too hot), and then cup your hands into the smoke and wash the smoke over your body. Hold the intention that cords are being purified and cleansed.

Using Feathers with Smoke

Another highly effective way to clear cords is to combine the movements of the feather with the use of smoke. These two elements together create an alchemy of air and fire that's a powerful way to cut cords and purify energy. The natural channeling powers of the feather, combined with the purifying and spiritual properties of the burning incense or herbs, can create a sense of deeply sacred space and healing.

To activate this alchemy, hold a bowl with the smoking herbs (or incense or sage bundle) in your nondominant hand. An abalone shell can also be used, but a deep bowl is a practical alternative that can be a little easier to manage. Make sure that the bowl or shell is deep enough to prevent any sparks or burning leaves from flying out of it into the room. You will also want to be sure that the bowl contains enough sand, salt, or earth to insulate it from the heat of the burning herbs, so that you don't burn your hand. Use the feather in your dominant hand to move the smoke over your body as you cut the cords. As mentioned before, use chopping, flicking motions, followed by long, sweeping ones to smooth out the energy after cleaving the cords.

Whenever you're using burning herbs, it's very important to take special precautions not to burn yourself or cause fires. Additionally, it's essential to take care that none of the burning embers land on carpets, furnishings, or clothing. Use an abalone shell or fireproof dish underneath the herbs to catch any stray sparks. And when you're through with your smudging ceremony, extinguish the herb bundle with water and leave it in a safe place such as a sink for a number of hours to make sure that it's truly out. Never leave a burning bundle of herbs unattended, and use water to completely extinguish them when you're finished. Many people have made the mistake of assuming a smudge bundle was out, only to come back later and find it smoldering once again.

Clearing Method 8: Salt

Salt is a powerful addition to any cord-release methods. And it's highly effective. It has been used throughout history and around the world because it has been universally recognized as a great purifier. Both sea salt and rock salt are excellent to use for clearing. Although their overall effects are the same, there are subtle differences between the two. Sea salt brings the energy of water and the ocean with it, so it's very effective for spaces dedicated to emotional healing. Rock salt comes from the earth and is more grounded in nature. It contributes to feelings of balance and integrity.

To use salt for releasing cords, first scrub your body in the shower or bath with salt, with the intention that the salt is scrubbing away and releasing what is not needed. Remember to end with a cold rinse. You can also take a salt bath before a cord-cutting ceremony.

Before utilizing any of the other methods of cord cutting—for instance, the scissors or knife method or the golden light—obtain a new container of table salt. Sprinkle a bit around the periphery of the room or space where you are going to do the cord release. Pay particular attention to the corners, which is where stagnant energy tends to accumulate. Then create a circle of salt to stand in while doing the cord ceremony. Immediately after the cord cutting, vacuum up and dispose of the salt. It's okay to pour it down the sink.

If you are outdoors, instead of using table salt, use Epsom salt. Regular table salt is not good for plants, but Epsom salt is a different mineral—magnesium sulfate—and will not harm plants. It also has amazing clearing properties.

After the salt clearing, take a cold shower. The frigid water will wash any leftover heavy, dark energies out of your energy field. Make sure that the water goes over the top of your head as well. It only takes a few minutes to clear out unwanted energies. If you can't shower, wash your hands in cold water up to the elbow and shake the water off vigorously over the top of your head before you dry your hands.

Another method to use *after* your clearing is to add a couple cups of Epsom salt (or a combination of equal parts table salt and baking soda) to your bath and soak for at least 20 minutes. You might want to add some essential oils such as pine or fir, as evergreens are cleansing and purifying. Although citrus and eucalyptus oils are also cleansing, for some people they can be an irritant in bathwater, so it is wise not to use them. When you step out of the bath, your energy field will be clearer. Additionally, the magnesium in Epsom salt can be absorbed transdermally into your body, so it also helps you relax.

Clearing Method 9: Waterfall Sweep

This is a highly effective yet simple technique. This one is especially potent if you don't have the time to do an intensive cord clearing. You can do this in a parking lot or in a public restroom stall. For example, if you are shopping in a crowded mall and suddenly feel your energy zapped, duck into the nearest restroom to do this clearing method. Begin with a quick scan to see the cords that are flowing out of you. Notice or be aware of them without judgment. Then take your hands and sweep them over the front of your body and sides with rapid strong movements. Use the sound "shu" out loud, and forcibly, again and again, with every swipe. As you do this, visualize the cords releasing and imagine that you are standing under a refreshing, bracing waterfall and everything that is releasing is flowing away. You don't have to be tucked away somewhere private to do this. I've done this in the lobby of a theater. Folks looked at me a little strangely, but I actually didn't care, as I felt so much better afterward.

Clearing Method 10: Breath of Fire

One formidable method for clearing utilizes your breath. To use this potent technique, take a few very deep, full breaths to center yourself. Imagine that you are breathing in *prana* (life-force energy) with every inhalation, and releasing all that is not needed with every exhalation. Then increase the rhythm of your breathing until it is very rapid. Once you sense that you have released stagnant cords, you can use long outflowing breaths to smooth and refine the energy. Your hands can follow the movement of air created by your breathing to enhance the effectiveness of this technique. Here is the step-by-step method:

1.   Stand with your legs at least a foot apart. Gently sway back and forth and side to side until you find the place where you feel very centered.

2. Relax your body and bend slightly at the knees. (In other words, unlock the knees.) Let your arms hang loosely at your sides.

3. Start with a few very deep, full breaths, and exhale loudly through your nose. (You may need to blow your nose before you begin this.)

4. Hold the intention of what or whom you desire to release. Breathe in life-force energy, and as you breathe out, release all that is not needed.

5. Slowly increase the rhythm of your breathing until it is very rapid. If you get dizzy, slow down for a bit until you feel balanced, and then gear up again. (This method is not recommended for someone with high blood pressure or glaucoma.) You should notice some strands just dropping off your body when you do this method.

6. To complete the process, slow your breath down and take very deep, very full breaths. You should feel lighter and brighter; when you look at your remaining strands, they should all be plump and bright and radiant.

Clearing Method 11: Bells

One of my very favorite methods of clearing cords is to use sound from such objects as bells, singing bowls, and gongs. Bells have the ability to shatter accumulated stagnant energy strands by producing a sound that permeates the molecules of a space and even penetrates the space between the molecules. The tone increases the flow of energy and restores vibrational balance. Concentric circles of sound continue to resonate long after we perceive that the tone has faded into silence. In almost a mystical way, the sound knows which of your strands need to be culled.

Historically, bells have often been associated with mysticism. Ancient metalsmiths believed that a kind of alchemy could be achieved during the bell-making process. In some cultures, bells were made of different metals, each of which was thought to carry the energy of a different planet, an idea originally posited by Aristotle. When such a bell was rung, it was believed to generate universal forces capable of aligning a dwelling space with the cosmos. Iron was associated with Mars because of its rusty red color and importance in ancient warfare. Lead, heavy and sluggish, was linked to Saturn. The metal mercury was associated with the planet Mercury because of its quick movements. Silver represented the moon, while the sun was gold. Emperors, such as Holy Roman Emperor Rudolf II, commissioned bells made of these metals and others, believing that they could inspire tremendous energy.

In some traditions, the ringing of metal bells was thought to drive away harmful spirits and negative energy. Hebrew rabbis rang bells before entering the most sacred areas of a temple to keep negativity at bay. In Medieval Europe, church bells rang out not only to call people to worship but also to dispel dark forces. At the same time that sacred bells were being crafted and used in Europe, they were also being used in the temples, monasteries, and ceremonies of Japan, China, Tibet, Indonesia, India, and the Middle East. In Buddhist cultures, the sound of the bell was an offering to the Buddha. Egyptian drawings on tomb walls show priests ringing bells to bestow blessings and dispel dark energies.

To release cords using a bell:

1. First, hold the bell to your heart. Fill it with love. Imagine the love spiraling around inside the bowl of the bell.

2. Hold the bell out a few inches from your body, parallel to your solar plexus chakra.

3. Ring the bell. If the striker, also called a clapper, begins to spin, this often indicates unbalanced energy. However, don't be concerned. Just keep ringing until it rings clear.

4. Finally, hold the bell parallel to your pubic bone—
   near your first chakra—and slowly lift the bell up and
   over your head. As you do this, hold the intention
   that unneeded strands are dissolving.

Balinese bells. There are many different types of bells; one very special bell is the Balinese bell. They are often used for clearing because of their superior tone. Perhaps part of the power of these remarkable bells comes from the fact that their creation is synchronized with the phases of the moon, with prayers and blessings to the gods offered at each step of the process. Making a Balinese bell can take two months or longer, but on the auspicious day when it's finally done, a beautiful consecration ceremony calls life into the newborn bell.

Tibetan bells. Tibetan bells (*ghanta*) are excellent tools for clearing cords and strands. Although they were originally made in Tibet, after the takeover of Tibet by the Chinese, Tibetan refugees have created these highly symbolic bells in Northern India and Nepal. Every part of a Tibetan bell is richly laden with meaning. The bell should come with a small metal object called a *dorje*, which represents the male principle, power, and salvation. The bell itself represents the feminine principle, wisdom, and the great void. Using the *ghanta* and the *dorje* together is thought to restore balance, because they represent yin and yang, the two opposing yet harmonious forces in the universe. Their combination creates an inner mystical unity, a balance of the two primordial creative forces of life.

Sometimes frightening faces are imprinted on the surface of Tibetan bells. These images of gods and goddesses are intended to dispel forces of evil and darkness. On the top of the bell is often a mandala of eight lotus leaves symbolizing the voices of the gods. Along the bottom edge of the bell are images of 51 *dorjes*, representing 51 challenges that can be resolved by the ringing of the bell. Traditionally, a lama would ring the bell while doing mudras (ritualistic gestures) with the *dorje*, which represented the dance of the gods. Tibetan bells can also be played in the same manner as a singing bowl, by circling a wooden mallet around the circumference of the bell.

In this chapter, you've learned some methods to unhook or release energy strands that are diminishing you. In the next chapter, you'll learn some protection techniques so that you are less likely to pick up strands that are not empowering.

Chapter Four

Protecting and Shielding Your Energy Field

Imagine you are in a sturdy cabin in the woods late at night; a tremendous storm outside is thrashing the trees, and thundering rain is pounding down on the roof. You are curled up in a large comfortable chair in front of the fire, absorbed in a good book, sipping a fine port, and listening to baroque music while the storm wails outside. You are supremely safe and content in your retreat. This is what it is like to have a strong protective energy around you. No matter what is occurring outside, you are sheltered, relaxed, and protected.

Energy protection is a very strong energy field around you that allows what is "yours" to be yours . . . and what is "theirs" to be theirs. Shielding techniques have been used over thousands of years in cultures around the world. In every native and ancient culture, the mystics, elders, priests, shamans, medicine men, and medicine women have maintained the importance of protecting one's energy. There is a very real reason for doing this that continues to be relevant in today's world.

In many ways, our energy fields can be likened to a crystal-clear swimming pool. If there isn't a fence around the pool, and all the neighbors and their friends swim in the pool, track mud into it, and even urinate in it, it will get murky. This is similar to our energy fields; if we don't have personal boundaries, our energy can get exceedingly dismal and dull.

We take protective measures in every area of our life. For example, to protect our physical bodies, we have seatbelts, smoke detectors, electrical plate covers, and guard rails, so it makes sense to protect and guard our life-force energy as well.

In this chapter, you'll learn when you might need energy protection and what deeper energies are at play, as well as some excellent psychic self-defense methods. We'll start by exploring whether protection is or isn't always a good idea—and why.

IS PROTECTION ALWAYS A GOOD IDEA?

Of course it's a good idea to guard your energy and keep it strong and clear. However, before you jump into activating a protective shield around yourself, there are some things to contemplate, as there are some very good reasons to *not* protect yourself. Here's why:

1. It affirms the illusion that we are separate from each other. The challenge with energy protection is that from a spiritual perspective, there is nothing out there that is not you (as I've mentioned before), so ultimately there is nothing from which to protect yourself. We are each connected to (and a part of) a living, pulsating Universe—one that sings with life and reverberates with the intensity of Spirit. There were no "bad" and "good" parts of creation. Everything is relative to everything else; nothing exists in isolation. You have an intimate connection with the firmament. And when you are connected to your source, there is never anything to fear; there is no need to shield yourself. So, from a spiritual perspective, shielding can create a barrier between you and the world. It affirms the illusion that we are separate from each other.

2. It can diminish compassion. Whenever you shield yourself from someone, you are declaring that you want a wall between you. For example, it's not uncommon for people to protect themselves when they are with someone who is dying. Of course the physical energy of the person who is dying is low. Their body's life force is draining away, and some people are worried that their energy will be drained as well. But far better than putting a shield around yourself is to connect with the soul of that person. When you connect with someone's soul (not their physical body and not their emotional body), there is only love . . . and *love never needs a shield*. This is true in any encounter.

To understand this, imagine that *you* were in a hospital, dying. Would you want those around you to be protecting themselves from you? Chances are this wouldn't feel good to you. What would feel great would be if each person saw your light and your soul and truly saw *you* . . . and not your dying body.

There are times when it's important to set aside your fear, and the feeling of the need to protect yourself, and to step into your strength, courage, and grace. Imagine that you notice your energy drop after an encounter. Before you activate your protective armor, take a moment to tune in to the essence of the other person. In other words, find the place within that person where their spirit and their love dwell—find the place where you are not separate from each other. This is holy. When you touch that place, there is no reason to protect yourself.

Many decades ago, when I looked into the eyes of the unknown gunman who had just hit me with his car and then shot me, and who was just about to shoot me again, the crazy thing was that, instead of feeling afraid, I saw his soul and felt a depth of compassion for him. I connected with the place in him in which we were not separate from each other. That was a sacred moment. I'm still amazed and in awe that this happened.

And although it felt like he really wanted to shoot me again, he couldn't do it. His arm trembled as he pointed the gun at me; it was as if an internal struggle was going on. Then he turned, got in his car, and drove off. It seemed that simply dissolving the barriers between us—and touching his soul—changed everything.

I didn't protect myself at a time when to not protect myself energetically seemed incredibly foolhardy, and yet it probably saved my life.

3. It can reinforce being a victim of life. Continually protecting yourself reinforces the idea of being a victim of life. It solidifies a belief that others can hurt or deplete you. Someone who constantly protects their energy is saying to themselves, "I'm the kind of person who needs protecting. There are a lot of things out there that can harm me." The trouble with this is that, subconsciously, you are affirming that there are people and situations that you need to constantly protect yourself from, and this can become a self-fulfilling prophecy. In other words, the more you protect yourself, the more things you will attract that you need to protect yourself from. This contributes to feeling that you are at the mercy of life's fortunes . . . and not in charge of your own destiny.

So there are some good reasons to not shield yourself, and protecting your energy field is not something to do in a frivolous manner. On a personal note, I very rarely shield myself. However, there are times when it's a very good idea to protect your energy field. For example, I protect myself when I forget who I am, and this usually occurs when I feel fear. If I'm walking at night alone in a part of town that I don't know and I feel afraid, I immediately cast a defensive energy armor over my body. Or if I am talking to someone who is overbearing, and I can feel my energy beginning to plummet, I immediately cast a protective shield over myself. I don't hesitate. And you shouldn't either. If you ever feel the need to place a shell of defense around yourself, do it.

Please don't judge yourself when you decide to shield yourself. Know that there are times when we feel spiritually expansive and there are times when we feel very human. It's important to honor both of these perceptions of self. If you are feeling human and vulnerable, and feel that you need to shield yourself, then do it without hesitation.

If your energy is up, everything is usually fine when you are around others. But if you have a day when your energy is lagging, you can be impacted by the energies around you, and you can feel depleted. Most likely, you have picked up or absorbed energy from other people. This doesn't necessarily mean that they are bad people. It just means that they are not a good match for your energy. (The great thing is that the opposite can occur. When you are with people who are a frequency match with you, your energy can be uplifted and can sparkle.) I suggest that whenever you feel the desire to protect your energy field, tune in and ask, "Is it for my highest good?" and then proceed accordingly.

IS THIS MINE OR SOMEONE ELSE'S?

Whenever we are with other people, our energy field is affected. Sometimes our energy goes up, sometimes it goes down, and sometimes it's neutral. However, it's often difficult to tell what energy is yours and what is someone else's.

If you were feeling great and then, after you go near someone, your energy drops, this can be a clue that you have picked up on their underlying feelings. If you move away from them and your energy increases, this is also a kind of validation that you had been influenced by their energy. (Please remember, this doesn't mean they are bad. They just aren't a frequency match for you at the time. Someone else might be around that same person and have their energy skyrocket into joy.)

I was a professional shiatsu practitioner in my younger years. Sometimes I would feel great before a session, but then when I would put my hands on my client, I would notice a complete shift in my emotional state. I might go from feeling joyous to feeling anxious, depressed, or angry . . . in an instant. When I first started doing bodywork, I thought everything I was feeling was mine, and I would find reasons in my life that could account for those emotions.

Saul came to my shiatsu studio for a session one balmy spring morning. When he arrived, I was bubbling with joy about the daffodils that had just bloomed outside the window. But when I placed my hands on Saul's back, suddenly I plummeted into a dark depression. It felt like I had been in a bright room and then someone switched the lights off. I scanned my life to see what had caused this instant depression. I thought things were going well in my relationship with my husband, but maybe there were issues I wasn't aware of. I thought about issues from my childhood and wondered if the depression was related to those. However, when I lifted my hands off Saul, the emotion dissolved. When I talked to Saul after his session, he told me that he had just lost his job and he was extremely depressed and upset about it.

Eventually, I began to understand that those sudden shifts of emotion I felt were my clients' emotions, not mine. To confirm this, I would ask the client how they were feeling, and almost always, they would affirm the emotions I was experiencing.

Feeling the emotions and thoughts of others is not uncommon. If you notice your energy drop around a particular person or in a particular location, chances are it is not your energy you are feeling. You have absorbed some of their energy. Have you ever . . .

- walked into a crowded shopping mall and felt exhausted afterward?

- worked all day with some challenging co-workers and felt drained by the end of the day?

- listened to someone's problems and felt depleted afterward?

- stood next to a stranger, perhaps in line at the store, and felt irritable afterward?

- had sudden stabbing pains in your stomach, seemingly out of nowhere?

- visited a hospital nursing home or jail and felt de-energized afterward?

- sat close to someone in a waiting room, at a gathering, or at a restaurant and had unaccounted for emotions afterward? (It's even possible to absorb the emotions of the person who prepared the food you ate at a restaurant.)

- felt as if a heavy blanket had been thrown over you?

- noticed that after having a few drinks at a party, different people seem to wobble your energy field?

- felt suffocated by a friend, acquaintance, or family member when they were talking with you?

These symptoms can often be a sign that you are absorbing or picking up energy from others in a way that's not beneficial to you. Sometimes there are influences that you can't see but that still affect your energy. Some locations have residual energy from past events that you can absorb. Have you ever walked into a room after there had been an argument, and the room felt thick? This is residual energy. And some locations have predecessor energy from people who lived there (or died there—as in an earthbound spirit) that can also lower your energy.

There are a myriad of visible and invisible forces that can unbalance your energy. Protection can be a good idea when energy that you absorb is not beneficial. Protection is also warranted at times when someone consciously (or even subconsciously) directs negative energy toward you. This is called a psychic attack.

PSYCHIC ATTACKS

Reports of psychic attacks have been chronicled throughout history in cultures around the world. These attacks can be powerful and can throw you into a tailspin, but they can also be subtle. In some cases, the attack can have been going on for so long that you aren't even aware of it. It's a bit like the force of gravity, which is constantly exerting pressure on you, but it's always been there, so it seems normal. Sometimes you are aware of a psychic attack only when it stops. For example, if the individual dies or if you do a release ceremony, you then might feel a shift. The constant drone of a continual psychic attack—for example, from a disgruntled family member—can be such a part of the fabric of your life that you are not aware of it. Once it releases, though, you will feel light and buoyant. Sometimes psychic attacks are deliberate and conscious, but most of the time, they are subconscious.

Subconscious Psychic Attacks

In a subconscious psychic attack, someone may subconsciously mount an attack by focusing negative thoughts at you, without doing it on purpose. Here's how most subconscious psychic attacks occur: Someone gets angry with you. They are thinking of you while they are mad . . . and you get a headache. They weren't conscious that they were doing this. It just was a by-product of their angst. But they can only affect you if there are energy strands connecting you to each other. Almost always, subconscious psychic attacks come from someone you know, someone with whom there are already cord attachments. There are times they can come from someone you don't know, but this is rare.

A subconscious psychic attack aimed toward you might manifest in a number of ways. You might wake up with a stomachache or you might suddenly feel upset for no reason. These symptoms can be natural occurrences, but it can also be that you were the subject of a psychic attack. You might even unintentionally send an attack to someone else. In my youth, I had a boss who I considered to be very unreasonable. One day, he accused me of something I didn't do. I was upset, but I didn't feel like I could tell him how distressed I was, so I didn't say anything about the incident. I just held my emotions down all day. However, when I went home that night, I exploded.

Seething, I said, "Damn him! I just wish a steamroller would roll over him." I even imagined his body looking like a cartoon, where he was as thin as a sheet of paper after he had been rolled over. It was a random thought. Of course I didn't want him to be harmed, but in the moment, it made me feel better to see him as a kind of cartoonish flat man after being rolled over again and again. Often when someone's emotions are suppressed, their thought forms become more potent, and I must have had very focused, strong thoughts because of what happened in the aftermath.

The next day I went to work and my boss looked terrible. I said, "What's wrong, Neal?" He replied, "I don't know what happened, but when I woke up this morning *I felt like I'd been run over by a steamroller.*"

I was shocked and felt terrible. I didn't mean to harm him, but evidently I had unconsciously sent him harmful energy, which is a kind of psychic attack. It was a misuse of energy, even if I didn't consciously know what I was doing. I vowed to never do something like that again. And I haven't—even if I'm angry with someone or about a situation. There have been a few times that I've been tempted, especially if someone I care about has been mistreated. I'm a bit like a mother bear in that regard. But so far, I've held off, because I know how powerful these psychic attacks can be.

The more personal power and inner strength you possess, the less likely you are to ever want to direct your anger toward another. People who send subconscious negative thought forms usually are people who feel disempowered or like victims in life. They lack personal power. The more likely you are to speak up for yourself, the less likely you are to send a subconscious negative thought form to someone. If I had told Neal that I was angry about the situation and calmly given him the reasons why, I wouldn't have had pent-up emotions that exploded into a kind of psychic arrowhead that penetrated him.

If you are smugly thinking that you've never sent a subconscious psychic attack to someone, ask yourself if you ever got mad at and sent an ill wish to an individual who . . .

- drove dangerously in traffic?
- squeezed in front of you to take your parking spot?

- elbowed their way in front of you in line?
- was rude on the phone with you?

If you answered yes, chances are there have been times that you subconsciously sent someone negative energy. Please don't feel guilty about it. We've all done it. It's important to forgive yourself. However, if you catch yourself doing it . . . stop immediately. These kinds of attacks always boomerang back to you, sooner or later, one way or another. Later in the chapter, you'll learn ways to repel psychic attacks and negative energy that boomerangs back to you.

Deliberate Psychic Attacks

Most psychic attacks are subconscious; however, in rare cases, there are some people who consciously send negative energy out. It can be hard to feel centered if this happens to you. In the past, these negative thought forms were called curses, spells, pointing the bone, or black magic, among other things. These kinds of attacks occur when someone is experiencing intense emotions and directs those feelings to one person with a focused, laserlike ferocity. They are real, but there are ways to fend off these attacks.

If you are the object of a directed and intentional psychic onslaught, but your energy is strong, nothing (and I mean *nothing*) can penetrate you. You won't even know that you are being attacked when it is happening. You will be on a different frequency. It's like you are tuned in to the classical station on the radio and even though, on another station, there's a shock jock ranting about the world, you'll never hear it. However, in times when you are tired, have ill health, are drinking a lot of alcohol or taking recreational drugs, or are going through emotional upheaval, your energy field might be thinner, and a psychic attack can be devastating.

Once, when I was in Australia, I was informed by an Aborigine friend that some of her clan members were "pointing the bone" at an author who claimed that her best-selling book about Aborigines was a true story when it wasn't. I wasn't in a position to do anything about it, so I just prayed for all concerned. Shortly after the bone was pointed at her, the author's son was in a serious automobile accident. He eventually was okay. The author didn't know that the bone was pointed at her; nevertheless, it seemed to have dramatically impacted her life. (Her book, which originally was listed as nonfiction, was later relisted as a novel, which in fact it was.)

The term *pointing the bone* means that an Aborigine takes a bone and points in the direction of someone they wish to harm; it is a kind of psychic attack. It is such a serious attack that in the past, it was not uncommon for Aborigines who were victims of this kind of psychic attack to simply drop dead, with no perceivable physical cause.

It has only happened a couple of times in my life, but I have been the victim of conscious psychic attacks. These kinds of experiences can come at you out of left field and can be very challenging. Often you don't know what hit you. Once a woman who had attended my seminars told me that she'd had a revelation that we were meant to teach together. She said it would help her career. I didn't know her, except that she had attended several of my events. I politely said that I taught alone, and I wasn't really set up to co-teach. She insisted that it was our karma to teach together. She said that she saw herself teaching groups of thousands of people around the world . . . and I was the one who was going to help her get there. I never want to dismiss anyone's dreams, but I knew that I wasn't the one to do this for her, so I gently demurred; it seemed that she understood. Then I put it out of my mind.

A week later, seemingly out of the blue, I started to have moments when I felt that I couldn't breathe. At other times, I felt that there was an intense constriction in my chest. It happened again and again. Each time, it came on suddenly. My health was fine, so I didn't know what was happening. Finally, I went into a deep meditation. I saw dense, thick, dark strands that had wrapped around my chest and were squeezing my ribs. No wonder I felt like I couldn't breathe! Then suddenly, the woman's face emerged. She looked enraged, almost apoplectic. As soon as I saw her face, I realized that I was under a psychic attack. I was surprised it was her; I had almost forgotten our chat.

I immediately began to remove the strands. They were incredibly dense and sticky, almost like tar. Every time I tried to pull one off, it would reattach. I had to raise my frequency and vibration high enough that they couldn't stick. Eventually, I detached them, but over the next few months, when I was tired or my energy was down, another wave of attacks would occur.

I was curious if these were conscious attacks or subconscious ones . . . so I did a bit of stealth work. When I found out that she had trained in black magic, I realized that the attacks were probably conscious.

I understood why she attacked me. It was upsetting for her when I didn't agree with her, especially when she felt it had been a revelation that I was the one to make her famous. I didn't like being attacked, but I understood the deeper motivation. Additionally, I realized that she had some borderline mental illness challenges. On the road to compassion, it's valuable to comprehend why people act the way they do. This makes it easier for you to forgive and let go.

I also had compassion for her because of the law of karma, which declares that whenever a person consciously sends out energy to harm another, it will multiply in intensity and come back around. I knew that what she was sending me would eventually harm her. It's the way of energy. *Always*, the person who sends out a psychic attack is diminished . . . sometimes beyond measure. It may not be immediate, but it does happen.

As much as it might feel good to get revenge or cause someone to feel the hurt they caused you, it will harm you. *Do not do it.* The higher up on the spiritual rung you are, the faster it will come back to you. It's what I call IK: instant karma. I want to mention this just in case you were thinking, *Boy, I sure would like to wobble my ex-boss! Maybe I could send him just a teeny weeny psychic attack?* It will boomerang back to you. *Don't do it!*

There were times that it felt so unfair that the woman was attacking me; I hadn't done anything wrong. But I reminded myself that there was a deeper truth, and when I turned everything around, I realized that I had a pattern of being treated unfairly that reached back into my childhood. I knew the attacks were an opportunity to deal with that pattern, so I didn't retaliate. I worked on myself to release that old pattern. I did also erect some stiff shields of protection though! And I just kept pulling off the sticky strands when they managed to make it through the shield. Eventually, the attacks stopped . . . and I never heard of her again.

Symptoms of a Psychic Attack

All of the symptoms that I am going to mention can have perfectly logical reasons and might have nothing to do with an attack. However, if you have a number of these, and there are not physical reasons for them, you might want to explore your strands to see if it is an attack.

- **Sudden pain.** It might recur in the same location or at the same time of day. Or the pain may come on very quickly and leave as quickly.

- **Fatigue and lethargy.** You feel drained and exhausted, seemingly for no reason.

- **Headaches.** You experience a sudden onset of headaches, sometimes even severe ones.

- **Feeling physically cold.** You have uncharacteristic chills, or the feeling that you just can't get warm.

- **Nightmares.** Unusual frightening dreams occur in your night hours. It's not uncommon for images of the attacker to appear in your dreams, or come in a symbolic form. For example, Donald—one of my students—kept seeing a frightening deer with long, sharp teeth in his dreams. He also saw a deer being born that had evil-looking red eyes. Donald finally realized it was a jealous co-worker with the last name Dearborn who was bringing his energy down. He was lucky that it was such an obvious dream; often dreams are more difficult to untangle.

- **Feeling like you are being watched.** There can be a feeling that there is someone beside you or someone you can see just out of the corner of your eye, but when you look, there is no one there.

- **Fuzzy thinking.** It feels like there is sawdust in your brain. It's hard to find the word you want and it's very difficult to concentrate.

- **Restricted breathing.** Every time you take a breath, it feels like it is constricted or difficult. It can also feel like there is pressure on your chest, like someone is sitting on you.

- **Heavy, depressed feeling.** You have uncharacteristic negative feelings about yourself. It can feel like there is pressure in your chest making it hard to breathe, or just a feeling of being depressed.

- **Strong and sudden emotions.** You feel upset without having any reason. Or you overly react to a situation that normally wouldn't bother you. It can feel like there is an urgency to your emotions.

This is just a short list, and of course, there can be many reasons for these experiences, but if you have these symptoms, and you feel like you are under attack . . . you might be.

Why Would Someone Attack You?

It can be daunting to believe that someone is thinking harmful thoughts about you. The first time I experienced it, I was a bit in shock. I knew that I was a kind, thoughtful person and didn't wish anyone any harm; I couldn't understand why anyone would want to harm *me*. Okay, I was naïve . . . very naïve. Life isn't always fair. Sometimes bad things do happen to good people. However, beneath the surface of life, we learn and grow from every experience, even the less-than-pleasant ones. Here are some of the reasons that someone might attack you:

Jealousy. Most of the time, an attack comes from someone who is jealous of you. Maybe you have advanced at work and they haven't. Maybe you married the person they desired. Maybe your sibling feels that a parent likes you more. Or maybe their life feels stagnant, while your life is sailing forward with joy. The list goes on and on. Jealousy is the most common reason for an attack. It's valuable to remember that *bad behavior comes from fear (or ignorance),* and if someone is jealous of you, chances are that at their core they are afraid of not being enough. It can help you develop compassion when you know that the person who is jealous of you is simply afraid and insecure.

Disagreements. Attacks can also come from someone who is upset that you don't agree with them about something—politics or religion, for example.

Mental illness. Someone who is mentally ill can't see the world around them clearly and can take offense at illusionary things. Their subconscious psychic attacks can be swift and vicious. I was in the unfortunate situation of having a mother who was diagnosed as paranoid schizophrenic. She was in and out of mental hospitals for many years during my childhood. She was violent at times, and some of the mental health authorities were worried about my safety. The strands between us were so durable that even if I was 500 miles away, I could feel when she was having an episode, especially when she was focused on me. The energy was so intense that sometimes I felt like I was getting slugged over the head with a baseball bat. (Her paranoia often caused her to believe that I was an enemy; at one point, she thought that I caused the Watergate episode with President Nixon. Another time she thought the FBI was watching me, and she walked up and down the sidewalk in front of our house with a sign that said, *I know that we are being watched.*)

Drug addiction. Someone who has a serious drug addiction not only has holes and tears in their auric field (so that astral entities can slip through to attach to them) but also—because they aren't seeing the world clearly—they can take offense where no offense was intended and can send a searing psychic attack to someone who they feel wronged them.

Possession. Although it is very, very rare, there are times when someone is possessed. However, 99.99 percent of the time, what we think is a possession simply isn't. You will probably never come across someone who is possessed in your lifetime. More often than not, a person is imbalanced or mentally ill but we assume they are possessed because of what we see in movies and television shows.

I have included possession under psychic attack because being possessed can feel similar. But it is different from an attack. Possession is when an entity (or even an earthbound spirit) co-occupies a body for a while. It can only happen if the body has openings in the auric field. These openings usually come from taking too many drugs (or too much alcohol) for extended periods; although sometimes it can occur if someone is exhausted or if they are always giving their personal power over to others.

Did I Draw This to Me?

Some people ask, "Did I attract this attack to me?" From a spiritual perspective, we draw all life experiences to us to learn and to grow. It doesn't mean that there is anything wrong with you. Nor does it mean that you are a negative person. It's just one of life's experiences. Please do not judge yourself if you become the victim of a psychic attack. You don't know the whole story. Just look at it as a learning experience.

Here is an example of not knowing the whole story. Six months after Barbara had taken one of my seminars, she made the decision to divorce her husband. She had been thinking about it for three years. Her husband was an abusive alcoholic, and she realized that she had been enabling him. She knew it was time to change her life. When she told her husband that she wanted a divorce, he decided it must be because of all the "New Age stuff" she was doing. As my course was the latest one that she had done, he decided that it must be my fault . . . and he flew into a rage that was directed at both Barbara and me.

Barbara was terrified of him and went into hiding. The folks at the domestic violence shelter in her town were worried about her safety and suggested that she leave the state while her husband cooled down. With his wife in hiding, the husband focused his fury against me. He would wait in his car outside our residence and then follow my car in an intimidating way. He wrote threatening letters, and hacked into my computer. At the same time as these things were occurring, I could feel the onslaught of his anger; it was a strong psychic attack. Eventually, my husband and I got a restraining order. We were given the strongest and longest one available in the state of California. I knew I hadn't done anything to this man. I had never counseled his wife to get a divorce. I would never do that; it wasn't my place. But instead of wondering what I had done to draw this experience into my life—and beating myself up—I told myself that I didn't know the whole story. I reminded myself that even if I didn't understand why I had gotten tangled up in someone else's dilemma, it was a part of the Creator's plan. And it really was.

After the three-year restraining order had expired, the husband wrote to me to profusely apologize . . . and also to thank me. He said the whole experience was the best thing that ever happened to him—it completely turned his life around. He had been one of California's premier executives in a global industry, but as a result of what occurred, he lost his job, his prestige, his wife, and his friends. Subsequently, he said, he did a lot of soul searching. He eventually went to massage school and became a healer. He realized he had become a successful businessman to fulfill his parents' expectations, but he didn't like being an executive. However, after he lost everything, he found his heart's calling in being a healer. He said that it never would've happened if he hadn't gotten the restraining order from me . . . that was the wake-up call that he needed.

Of course, I had my own journey, and I grew through it all as well. In the past, I had been afraid to stand up for myself, so one of the things that I gained was being willing to take a stand when I went to court to get the restraining order. I share this experience with you as a reminder that often we don't know the whole story, even when we feel that we are being psychically attacked. Although there is usually a deeper purpose at play, there is still immense value in learning how to shield and protect your energy in the event that you find yourself the recipient of unwanted energies.

Consider Your Own Part in the Psychic Attack

We each bear some responsibility if we are psychically attacked. From a higher perspective, it's something that we put into motion or something that we opened ourselves up to. At times, we have attracted it into our lives as a way of growing spiritually. Sometimes just admitting that you bear some responsibility can de-escalate the situation. It's like when there is an argument, and then one person apologizes, it often defuses everything.

Even though, on some deep level, you have attracted the situation into your life, as I mentioned previously, there is never any reason to feel guilty about it. You are growing spiritually. Sometimes the lesson that you are learning is to stand up for yourself and take action. At first, I was horrified about getting a restraining order. I was embarrassed and even ashamed. I figured that if I had attracted being stalked into my life, I should take responsibly for it. And I felt guilty about attracting it into my life. But with deep introspection, I realized that I had never stood up for myself in my life. I never made waves. I was always trying to keep the peace at any cost. The restraining order was the first time in my life that I stood up for myself. It was a powerful life lesson, and from that point forward, I have felt stronger and more confident in myself. So both the man and I gained from the experience.

"TRUST IN GOD, BUT TIE UP YOUR CAMEL"

Even if you don't believe in protection techniques, and you know that love is the greatest protection, and you believe that the angels will always shield you, it's still valuable to know how to protect yourself. Be willing to take action in the rare event that you need to. In life, we can trust in Spirit, but it's also valuable to take positive steps to protect ourselves.

So, if you are considering taking a shortcut through a dark alley in a dodgy area of town and think everything will be okay because you've shielded yourself, remember you need to do your part too. Sometimes energy protection isn't enough; you have to also take action . . . and perhaps don't take the shortcut.

I believe in seeing the world in the best possible way and being optimistic in life. However, I also believe the Middle Eastern expression, "Trust in God, but tie up your camel." What does this mean? It means to trust that all is well; however, even though you trust God to watch over your "camel," it is your job to also tie him up for the night so he doesn't wander off. You need to help out too.

Trust in the qualities of light, gratitude, and joy. But in the rare event that you are the victim of a psychic attack, it's good to be prepared to take action. I think it's like trusting that you will have a wonderful journey in your car and surrounding your car in white light, but also using your seatbelt. You are prepared in the event that there is an accident. You've taken physical action as well as spiritual action.

One night, as I was just about to drift off to sleep, I remembered that I had forgotten to close the door to the chicken coop. It was cold outside, and I was so warm in bed. I thought, *It will be okay. I'll ask the angels to protect the chickens.* I called on Archangel Michael to stand at the door to the coop to protect the chickens during the night. I trusted that all was well.

In the early morning, I dreamed about three small piles of black feathers outside the chicken coop. The dream startled me and I threw on a robe and ran up the hill to the coop. Just as in my dream, there were three piles of black feathers . . . and when I went into the coop, our rooster, Gatsby, wasn't there. A coyote had gotten him in the night, and all that was left were the three piles of feathers. Gatsby was a gentle rooster, a gentleman—that's why we named him Gatsby. And he was gone, simply because I didn't "tie up my camel." It's a lesson that I've never forgotten. It wasn't enough to call upon the angels. I should have also taken action.

Sometimes thinking that nothing will happen, or thinking that the angels will protect you, isn't enough. Sometimes you need to be proactive. It's okay to protect yourself if you feel that you need it. In addition to the physical actions you can take to stay safe, there are some very valuable techniques that anyone can use to help protect your energy field, so that you feel centered and strong no matter who is around you.

PREPARATION FOR PROTECTION AND PSYCHIC SELF-DEFENSE

Here are some tips for preparing to protect yourself. Do these steps before any shielding method you choose.

1. Tune in. Every morning, take a moment to center and ground yourself. Tap into the place within you where deep and profound peace dwells. Connecting with that place allows your energy field to be stronger and more vibrant during the day.

Throughout the day, take time to raise your awareness and sense your energy fields by asking, "What is true for me now?" The soul loves the truth, and this spiritual practice can help you be aware of the strands and cords of energy around you. Take time to periodically notice the people you are with and the environment you are in. Notice if there are parts of your body that feel affected. It's important to get this baseline. As you get used to doing this, you'll know better when to protect yourself and when not to.

2. Distance yourself. When you discover someone or something that lowers your energy . . . step away. Rather than immediately raising your shield, sometimes simply putting some physical distance between you and the other is enough. Create a personal boundary through space. You can also disassociate emotionally.

Don't react and don't take things personally. Detach yourself—it's not about you. Don't feed their drama. Often your own negative response to someone can hurt you more than their negativity. Change the focus of your conversation. If they start moaning about Cousin Billy in a negative way, talk about the roses you saw on the way to work. If they want to talk about their problems, shift the focus to supporting them in finding solutions. It usually doesn't work to try to change another person's perception, but you can respond rather than react.

3. See through the eyes of the other. Facing the deeper truth is not always easy. Imagine that you are looking at the world through the eyes of the person from whom you feel you may need to protect yourself. Even though it's hard, try to see their point of view. You don't need to accept it; you simply need to understand it. The more you can have compassion and understanding of the person you feel is draining your energy, the less they will be able to deplete your energy. This exercise softens the polarity between the two of you.

4. Visualize your day. Take time to visualize your day and see yourself relaxed and energized throughout the entire day. Twenty-four minutes is the optimum amount of time to take to do this—one minute for each hour. However, even 60 seconds of visualization can make a difference. Be positive. Focus on things that make you feel great. Immediately check yourself if you find you're dwelling on lack or worry for the day during your visualization. Deliberately change your state of mind, and delete limiting thoughts. Shift to something that brings you joy. This exercise keeps your energy vibrant throughout the day, and thus you are less likely to need shielding.

METHODS FOR PROTECTION
AND PSYCHIC SELF-DEFENSE

Whenever you are with other people, your energy field is affected. It's often difficult to tell what's yours and what is someone else's. However, there are some very valuable techniques that anyone can use to help protect your energy field if needed, so that you feel centered and strong no matter who is around you. My suggestion is to try them all to find out which one works best for you.

Protection Method 1: White Light

Often, when we see paintings of saints, they have a glow around them or a radiant halo. Sometimes this light is called Christ consciousness. It represents beneficial, positive energy. In *The Wizard of Oz*, Glenda, the good witch, shows up in a radiant bubble. All that is good is in the bubble. For this protection method, you are creating your own bubble of dazzling white light. Visualizing a sphere or ball of white light in which to encompass yourself is one of the most common and effective ways of protecting your energy.

Visualize that any energies that are not needed simply deflect or bounce off the sphere. The effectiveness of this method depends on the clarity of your intention and your ability to focus and direct that intention. Simply imagining a ball of white light surrounding you can be efficient in most normal situations, but when creating a powerful, protective force field, here are some things that can help magnify its effectiveness.

1. Imagine an egglike sphere surrounding your body. It should project out from your body no less than a foot and no more than three feet in all directions. Eighteen inches is usually a good standard. It is filled with sparkling white light.

2. The sphere has a very strong surface; it can be compared to bulletproof glass. You can see through it, but it is very durable.

3. Check the entire surface for any small tears, cracks, or even wrinkles. Also, notice if there is any thinning of this shielding material. Ideally, the surface should be as smooth and reflective as a highly polished mirror.

4. If there is anything that needs repair, imagine that you have some cosmic glue or a magic wand to fix it. The outer surface should be so smooth and slick that nothing can attach to it.

5. Be aware that only the highest and finest beneficial energies can come through the strong, but semipermeable lining of your white light sphere. Your energy can flow out of it, but only the most pristine frequencies can come into it. It is an invisible, formidable force field.

You can use other colors besides white for your orb. You can imagine a sphere of pink light around you, which encompasses you in a loving energy. Or visualize an orb of green light, which embraces you with healing energy. Golden light often connotes the heavenly realms as well as inner wisdom. Or your sphere can be violet colored, moving from the negative to the positive. Imagine that you are in the center of a sparkling, glistening violet light. The violet light has the ability to transmute and dissolve dark energy into the light. It can help you release challenging energy from your past. It can also transform fear and angst into love and delight. All that is not needed is dissolving as this shimmering light surrounds you.

Sometimes it's helpful to imagine a semipermeable opening at the top of your sphere through which white or golden light cascades from the heavens and radiates down through you. Only heavenly light-force energy can come through the opening. And at the bottom of your orb is one-way drain, so all that is not needed can empty into the ground and be neutralized. Nothing can come back into this opening except that which is for the very highest good.

Many years ago, I had a friend who told me that the white light saved her life. She was crossing the road when a car came barreling straight toward her. She said, "Denise, I didn't have time to run, so I threw my hands over my head, grabbed white light and drew my hands down, as if closing a shade. Instantly, I was encased in white light."

She continued, "The car skidded to an immediate halt and stopped just at the edge of my white light shield. The driver got out—he was really shaken—and he was incredulous. He said that it felt like he hit some kind of invisible force field that stopped his car."

"What happened? I could've killed you!" he exclaimed. My friend told him about the white light, but he went away shaking his head in disbelief.

I'm sharing this with you because I want to let you know how powerful the white light protective sphere can be. However, from my perspective, if a car is racing toward you, run—don't walk—to get out of the way. A great idea is to "white light yourself" before you go out for the day, if your intuition warrants it.

Protection Method 2: Talismans

A talisman is something you place on your body, either around your neck, in a pocket, or in something you carry with you (such as a purse) that has objects in it that have protecting properties. They are often hidden but they can also be on outward display.

Amulets and talismans with the specific purpose of protection are common in most religious and spiritual traditions. Christians use the cross and rosary, Muslims use the *hamsa,* shamans in native cultures have medicine bags or medicine bundles filled with sacred objects that all serve as a protective force. Every native culture has a tradition of using talismans. In ancient burial sites throughout the world, archaeologists have found amulets that were thought to be used for protective purposes, even into the afterlife. In ancient Egypt, amulets were put on the dead to protect them as they traveled to the underworld.

Although, in Western cultures, we don't have a strong tradition of amulets and talismans, even in modern times they are used. When someone wears a lucky charm, or carries a rabbit-foot, this is an echo of carrying a protective amulet from earlier times. I was at a funeral for a Navajo Native American recently. It was a Christian service, but my friend's medicine bag was placed with him in the casket for protection on his journey into the afterlife, along with a large Christian cross. When astronaut Edward

White went to the moon, he carried with him a gold cross, a Star of David, and a Saint Christopher medal.

A modern-day talisman can be something that was blessed by a holy person, or it can be a stone or crystal that you have cleansed and blessed for protective purposes. It can also be a small object from a beloved relative, such as a grandparent or an ancestor, that is meaningful to you. It can also be herbs, such as sage or rosemary, which are traditionally used for protection.

Even a small stone in a necklace or in a purse or pocket can help create a protective shield around you. Here are some stones that are often used as protective talismans:

- Black tourmaline, black obsidian, Apache tears, onyx, smoky quartz, bloodstone, and jet are all excellent to repel energies that are not beneficial. These are the best stones to use to protect from heavy energies.

- Amber is excellent for protection from negativity. (In ancient times, the Romans used amber extensively for this purpose.)

- Halite (rock salt crystals) is superb for grounding and protecting. If you live in a humid area, keep your halite in a small plastic bag so it doesn't "weep" and stain your clothes or purse.

- Agates of all kinds have been used to dispel negative energy. You should pick out your own agate; choose one that feels powerful, because the protective qualities are not consistent from stone to stone in agates. Blue lace agate is excellent for children.

- Celestine, malachite, and quartz crystal can create a soft, loving orb of energetic shelter. (These are all also excellent for children and the elderly.) These are gentle and should be cleansed periodically, especially the crystal. (To cleanse a crystal—or any of these stones—run it under cold water for three minutes, or leave it outdoors under the stars and moon overnight or in a rainstorm for three hours.)

Talismans are believed to hold great power, but they react to your intentions and your beliefs. If you believe an item contains potent energy, then it will offer protection. If you believe that it doesn't, it won't. In my time in native cultures, I've been offered objects of power. It is an honor to receive them. Once, I was given the dried afterbirth of a reindeer that brought strength and protection to a Laplander shaman. It was special gift, and I knew that this object was powerful for the shaman, but to me it looked dried, ugly, and unsanitary . . . so it didn't hold a safeguarding energy for me. I didn't believe in its power; hence, it had none for me. Another Native American showed me that in his medicine bag, he had scalps from men he killed in Vietnam. He said they were part of his protection, but I was horrified. For me, these would have had negative energy, but for him, they were an attribute of being a strong warrior. When choosing items for your protection, notice your beliefs about the objects and be very clear on your intention for the amulet.

To get started:

1. Make or purchase a small bag or pouch to keep under your clothing where it can't be seen. Three inches by three inches is a good size. It can hang on a cord around your neck, be kept in a pocket or your purse, or can hang off your belt.

2. Decide what objects you want to place in your protection pouch. I suggest starting with a piece of obsidian and some dried sage. Over time, you can add other objects, or even written words on paper, such as *Archangel Michael protects me.*

3. Bless the bag by holding it to your heart and saying three times, "I am safe and protected. All is well."

Protection Method 3: Shielding

When I was in the outback with the Aborigines of Australia, I was given a "woman's shield." It was a narrow piece of wood— about six inches wide and two feet long. I couldn't imagine that it could shield anyone in a battle, as it was so small. However, I was told that as soon as a woman held it, her energy was shielded. It activated a kind of force field around her. When I heard this, I understood. Shielding yourself is creating a field of energy around you in which you are safe and protected. (It's different from the white light sphere, because it is an actual, physical shield.) Shielding doesn't mean you're closing your heart, and it doesn't mean you are disconnecting or shutting yourself from others. It does mean that you have very clear boundaries. Putting your shield up will help you avoid getting caught in the drama of another person. Your intention isn't to separate yourself from others; your intention is to continue to stay in your own energy. By shielding, no matter where you are, you're in your own energy field and not mingling with the energies of others.

Remember the phrase, "What is mine is mine; what is yours is yours."

People who are empaths especially need energetic shielding. An empath feels everything from everyone. It's like they've left their front door open and folks they don't even know are dropping in, sleeping in their beds, eating their food, leaving their garbage, and even moving in. If you are an empath, learning how to shield yourself can be the equivalent of locking the gate into your yard, so that only your energy is contained in your garden and in your home. Shields up!

Anytime you feel the need for shielding, imagine that you are holding a shield in front of you. You might imagine a Roman type of shield, a Viking shield, a Native American buffalo skin shield, or even Wonder Woman's shield! You can hold your hand in a fist at your solar plexus as if you were holding a physical shield. You can also imagine placing your shield around you before sleep, so that it provides a dream shield, containing your energy while you sleep.

To create your personal shield:

1. **Imagine a shield.** Visualize a shield similar to the shields that a Knight of the Round Table may have had, but made of light and energy. It is incredibly strong but lightweight. The energy radiating from the shield surrounds your entire body. The shield can be clear, silvery, golden, or even decorated with gems, such as rubies.

2. **Visualize symbols.** In your mind, place symbols on the shield that feel protective and powerful to you. Some people put crosses on their shield to represent the Christ light, some put hearts to symbolize love, some put a pentagram; others put images of gods or goddesses (such as Kali or Kwan Yin). Imagine your shield in any way you choose. If it helps, you can also make a drawing of your shield to enhance your visualization. You can keep your drawing between your mattress and box spring to deepen and strengthen your shield during sleep.

3. **Bless and empower your shield.** Go on an inner journey with your shield. To activate its power, imagine holding it up to the heavens to activate the spirit of air within it. Then visualize rain—the waters from heaven—cascading over it, imbuing it with the spirit of water. Now imagine that lightning strikes it, bringing forth the strength of the spirit of fire, and lastly, imagine holding it to the earth to activate the spirit of earth. Then take your shield and hold it to your heart to imbue it with the energy of love. You now have a very powerful shield.

Protection Method 4: Mirrors

There are several mirror ball protection techniques, and they all are excellent.

1. For protective shielding, imagine that you are inside a mirrored ball. The exterior of the ball is a shiny, slick, mirrored surface. Only positive energy of the highest frequency can enter; everything else reflects back. This works especially well for psychic attacks.

2. Another method is to imagine that you are surrounded by a ball of energy, *but the mirror is on the inside.* This way, your energy bounces back to you and doesn't seep away. It stays contained. You are in your own energy field. (You can also have both a mirrored inner surface and a mirrored outer surface.)

3. This third method is only for the most serious of cases. It's highly effective but should be used sparingly. If there is someone who is very overbearing and you just can't seem to keep your own energy field intact around them, this is what you might use. *It must be used with compassion and not out of anger or fear.* This is important, because you are directing this at another person rather than focusing on yourself.

    For this method, imagine that a mirrored ball (with the mirror on the inside) surrounds the person you feel victimized by. If they send out loving, joyous energy, it bounces back to them magnified. If they send out unkind energy, it also is magnified and bounces back to them. So any less-than-positive energy (that they may send to you) stays inside the mirrored ball.

Protection Method 5: Crystals

Crystals have been used in cultures around the world for protection and for energy activation. Here are the steps to using crystals for protection:

1. Choose the right crystal. To help you decide the size and shape of your stone, determine if you are going to . . .

- wear your protective crystal
- keep it in a medicine bag
- simply have it near you
- sew it into your pillowcase
- tape it to your solar plexus (with medical tape)

Then decide if you are going to use a polished, faceted crystal, a natural stone, or one that has been tumbled. When shopping for a protective crystal, it's best to let the stone choose you. What this means is that when you are picking one out, notice the crystal that seems to call you to it. It will seem somehow shinier and brighter than all the rest.

2. Cleanse your crystal. Leave it out in the sun for five hours or rub it in one direction with eucalyptus oil. Alternatively, washing it with peppermint soap and cold water will also cleanse it. Crystals have a very fluid energy and thus need to be cleansed often. (Other stones, like jet or obsidian, don't need to be cleared very often.)

3. Dedicate your crystal. Hold it up to your third eye and say, "I dedicate you to protection and strength. I am safe, protected, and well."

4. Use your crystal. Hold your crystal in your dominant hand and sweep it over your body three times. Make sure you go over the top of your head and also the sides of your body as well as down your front. (When you take the crystal over your head, hold the intention that the sweep goes down your back as well.) If you need extra protection, sweep it over your body nine times. This method will encompass you in a cocoon of safety and protection.

Protection Method 6: Sea Salt

Since the beginning of recorded history, there have been accounts of salt being used for protective purposes. Of all the things used for protection around the globe, salt is the most ubiquitous. It is used for safeguarding in every corner of the world. In some cultures, it is sprinkled along windowsills to keep out negative energies. In other cultures, the floors of a new home are sprinkled with salt and then the salt is swept out; it's believed that the salt absorbs dark energies, which then are swept out the door. Some societies have traditions of keeping salt in a person's pocket as a protective measure. Even in modern times, we have a tradition of throwing salt over our shoulder to fend off unwanted energies.

To use salt for protection, you can place a small chunk (or a few granules) of it in your medicine bag, or carry a small amount tied in a black silk bundle in your handbag. You can sprinkle a circle on the floor around your bed to sleep in its protective energy at nighttime. Alternatively, you can place a small amount of salt in the corners of your home to create a protective energy there. If you live in a humid environment, the salt should be placed in small containers; otherwise, it will attract and release fluid, which can leave salt stains on your floors or furniture.

You can also use salt lamps—these are made of carved-out natural salt with a lightbulb inside—to create a protective energy in the space where they are placed. These salt lamps are said to emit beneficial negative ions, which are cleansing for the air.

Protection Method 7: Adopt a Protection Tree

Trees can offer an incredibly sheltering force, especially if you have attuned to one's energy. You can adopt a tree in your yard, your neighborhood, a local park, or on a walking trail. Choose one that calls to you; then create a connection. To do this, lean or sit against that tree for at least 15 minutes and send love and gratitude into the tree. Imagine that the tree has a voice, and listen to what it tells you. As you build a relationship with your adopted tree, talk to it and give it heartfelt thanks. An energy bond is then created between you and the tree. Those who can see energy will be able to detect the beautiful, large cord of light between the two of you. Anytime you need protection, simply think of your tree, and the cord will plump and your energy will be grounded and strong.

It might sound strange, but one of the fastest ways to clear your energy is to either hug a tree or put your back up against a tree and allow the healing energy of the tree to cleanse and ground you. This works especially well if it is a tree you have a relationship with. Meditating near it or simply putting your hands on it will encase you in a sphere of protection and grace.

Protection Method 8: Essential Oils for Energetic Shielding

In addition to their cleansing properties (discussed in Chapter 3), essential oils are excellent to use for protective purposes. When I'm going into a situation where I feel the need for a protective mantle around me, I use essential oils. And also, as a general rule, I usually carry a small bottle or two in my purse so I always have some with me. The olfactory sense is closely connected to our emotional system, more so than any of our other senses. When we use essential oils, a powerful link is created between our physical realm and the psychic realm. That link is grounding and protecting. In many cultures, essential oils are used for protection. For example, the Sherpa in Tibet use juniper to rub into their ropes to help protect them on their treks.

Here's how you can use oils for protection: You can rub them in your hands and inhale. I usually place three drops into my palms, rub my palms together, cup my hands over my nose, and then inhale three times, with the intention of guarding my energy. Then I use my hands as a kind of fan and brush the scent over the top of my head and down my body. I also go over the back of my head, with the intention of sweeping the back of my body with the protective scent. This encompasses my entire body in a protective shield. Sometimes I will place one drop on my throat, one on my third eye, another on top of my head, and a fourth at the base of my skull, all to deepen the protection. An oil diffuser can be very useful when protecting a larger space or several people at a time.

You can also mix essential oils with water and use a mister (similar to what you would mist your plants with) to spray your body and/or your clothes. I often travel with a very small mister to keep a protective mantle around me on my journey. It cleanses and uplifts my energy and can protect it as well.

When choosing which oils to use, remember that within your soul is an innate wisdom that absolutely knows what oils are best for the particular protection that you need. So take time to tune in to your inner knowing before you choose your oils.

Note: While essential oils are a natural substance, some people have skin reactions when in direct contact with essential oils, especially on the delicate skin of the face. Always use care when putting oils directly on the skin. Essential oils can be mixed with carrier oils, such as jojoba, carrot, apricot kernel, or sweet almond, if you have sensitive skin and wish to use them directly on your body.

Here are some oils you can use for protection—most are good for both clearing and protection:

- **Basil**: herbal, sweet, fresh, green. Blends well with lemon, lemongrass, orange, rose.

- **Chamomile**: soft, warm, gentle (good for protecting children). Blends well with rose, lavender, ylang-ylang, neroli.

- **Cedarwood**: earthy, woodsy, warm. Blends well with sage, cypress, frankincense.

- **Cypress**: warm, soft, woodsy. Blends well with frankincense, peppermint, cedarwood.

- **Clove**: woodsy, earthy, warm. Blends well with cinnamon, cardamom, orange.

- **Eucalyptus**: fresh, clean, stimulating. Blends well with lemon, peppermint, thyme.

- **Fir**: fresh, clear, woodsy, green. Blends well with neroli, citrus oils, pine, juniper.

- **Frankincense**: warm, woodsy, sweet. Blends well with rose, cedarwood, myrrh, sandalwood.

- **Juniper**: woodsy, green, fresh. Blends well with evergreens (such as fir and pine), rosemary, vetiver, clary sage, lemongrass.

- **Myrrh**: warm, earthy, spicy. Blends well with frankincense, clove, sandalwood.

- **Orange**: fresh, clean, sunny. Blends well with thyme, eucalyptus, other citrus oils.

- **Patchouli**: warm, earthy, woodsy. Blends well with bergamot, clary sage, peppermint, geranium.

- **Peppermint**: fresh, cool, clean. Blends well with grapefruit, rosemary, eucalyptus.

- **Rosemary**: clear, fresh, spicy. Blends well with citrus oils, tea tree, peppermint, fir.

- **Sage**: woodsy, earthy. Blends well with citrus oils, cedarwood.

- **Vetiver**: warm, woodsy, earthy. Blends well with pine, basil, rose geranium.

There are many other essential oils you can use for energy protection, but these are some of the basics.

Protection Method 9: Meditation and Visualization

Almost any kind of visual meditation will strengthen your energy field. For example, close your eyes, relax, and imagine you are in a lush place in nature. Surrounding you is the brightest, most radiant light you've ever seen . . . "See" it grow in intensity and power. Imagine strands of energy from the stars, the sun, and the earth flooding into the light as it grows even brighter and more sparkling . . . with you at the center point. As you open your eyes, hold on to the meditation by trusting that this incredible light will continue to surround, protect, and safeguard you. This meditation works well for protection because you are so bright nothing can penetrate your energy force field.

As a daily practice, take a moment to ground and center yourself every morning. A good way to do this is to imagine a cord of energy flowing from the bottoms of your feet into the earth. Then, in silence, sink into the place of profound peace within you. Doing this allows your energy field to be stronger and more vibrant during the day.

Here is a fun, easy, effective protection method using visualization. Imagine that there is a cosmic zipper in front of you, starting at the base of your feet. Imagine zipping your energy field into an energy sphere; as you zip all the way up and over your head, you can leave a small opening at the top to allow celestial energies to flow down around you.

You can also place your hand near your pubic bone and imagine that you are holding a large zipper there; then physically move your hand all the way up to the top of your head to zip up and encompass your energy.

Protection Method 10: Prayers and Mantras

Saying a protective prayer can give you an immediate connection to the Divine. For some, the Lord's Prayer does this. For others, a prayer to Christ, Mother Mary, Allah, Buddha, or Yemaya works. Saying a prayer to whatever your spiritual source is, with the intention of safeguarding your energy, works.

Whenever we get into our car for a long journey, we say a prayer. It seems like a simple, almost childlike prayer, but we are safe and protected after we do it. Here's the travel protection prayer:

Angels in front of us; angels behind us.
Angels to the left and right of us.
Angels above and below us.
We are safe, protected, and well.

And then we visualize the wings of angels surrounding each occupant of the car. Another prayer I use is the Japanese mantra *"Namu Amida Butsu."* For me, this is powerful and immediate protection. I lived in a Zen Buddhist monastery for several years, so I have an affinity to Buddhism, and *Amida* is one of the loftiest ideals in Japanese Buddhism. Loosely translated, this mantra means *I take refuge in the light.* I've experienced miracles using it. One time, my husband, David, and my daughter, Meadow, and I were in our small car in the winter, driving through the Cascade Mountains. We hit an ice patch, and our car spun around and was careening to the edge of a sheer cliff. I shouted, *"Namu Amida Butsu!"* and the car stopped almost instantly . . . about a foot from the cliff. It was an incredible moment.

Another time, I was sitting in a small coffee shop with a friend, Katie, in San Luis Obispo, California, when a magnitude 6.4 earthquake hit. The floor began to roll and things were falling off the shelves. I grabbed Katie's hands from across the table, looked into her eyes, and began to chant, *"Namu Amida Butsu!"* Even though things were crashing down around us, we experienced a calm serenity. Katie said that the moment felt holy to her. It certainly did to me.

Protection Method 12: Mudras

A mudra is a way of holding your body that initiates a particular kind of energy. Many cultures use mudras to activate different kinds of energy. A shielding mudra is created by standing tall—weight equal on each leg—then clenching your hands into fists and crossing your arms at the wrist across your chest with force. Do this three times, each time with force, and your energy will be shielded.

Also, there are subconscious mudras that are protective. Simply holding your arms over your solar plexus is a kind of mudra, and it protects your solar plexus from negative strands. You'll notice this is something that people do automatically if they are in uncertain situations. If you are someplace where you feel your energy sagging, simply cross your arms over your solar plexus.

Protection Method 13: Angels, Guides, Spirit Guardians, and Ancestor Protectors

Those in the spirit realm love to offer assistance and keep you safe. Simply call upon your angels, spirit guides, and guardians, and instantly there can be help available. Call upon Archangel Michael to surround you with protective, loving energy. Imagine that huge, powerful Archangel Michael is standing behind you with his sword of light, protecting you and keeping you safe. His wings of light are embracing you and holding you in a cocoon of safety, no matter where you are or where you go.

In Western culture, the power of our ancestors is undervalued. However, in cultures that revere and honor their ancestors, their forebears are their most powerful advocates and protectors. You share the bloodline of your ancestors. They want to support you. Utilizing the protective abilities of your ancestors is simply a matter of asking. You can humbly say, "I call upon my ancestors, from the beginning of time and forward, for support and safeguarding." Alternatively, if there is a particular ancestor you knew or were close to when they were alive, you can call upon them. For example, you might declare, "Uncle Joe, you never took any guff from people when you were alive, and I admired that about you. I'd love your help so I don't continue to be upset by the guff I get at work. Help me stand in my own energy. Thank you so much!"

When you call upon your spirit helpers, remember to always give thanks. Usually you can feel their help immediately. In Chapter 5, I'll share more information about how to call angels into your home and into your life.

Protection Method 14: Earthing Yourself

In Chapter 1, you learned about the various strands of energy that we have connecting us to the earth and all of nature. Beyond simply offering connection, Mother Earth's energy can protect you and ground you.

Simply lie on the earth, either on your back or on your stomach, and imagine that you are giving your challenges to Mother Earth. Visualize tendrils of her energy lovingly reaching up and surrounding you with strength. Call upon her consciousness to surround you with a grounded, mighty mantle of protective energy.

You can also stand barefoot on the earth, or place your hands on the ground, to do this. Walking barefoot on wet sand, near the ocean, can dispel negative energies and can strengthen your energy field. If you are not able to easily get outdoors, simply use a houseplant for earthing. Touch its leaves to ground your energy. If the energy being cleared is very dense, it may have a depleting effect on your plant. So watch carefully to notice if your plant begins to wane. You may need to give it time to recover before using it again.

By earthing, you are literally plugging in to the earth's electrical field, and you will feel her neutralizing all that is not needed in your energy field. Mother Earth is the ultimate healer, and she can synchronize your biological rhythms and fill your body with negatively charged ions. It really works. In native cultures, it's believed that when one feels out of sorts, simply lying on the earth brings things into balance. When you are in balance, your energy field is strong; thus, there is a protective mantle around you.

All of the above methods work. It's simply a matter of trying each one out to see what works best for you.

SUBCONSCIOUS SHIELDING

There are some people who never do any protection methods, yet they are naturally shielded. Caregivers, hospice workers, hospital staff, and teachers sometimes find that their energies are depleted by those around them, unless they have developed natural (often subconscious) shielding methods. If you work in an area where most feel depleted and you don't, it may be that you have very strong spirit helpers or you have developed a kind of subconscious shielding that keeps you in balance, especially in those times when your energy is low.

WHAT DO YOU DO AFTER YOUR ENERGY FIELD HAS BEEN DIMINISHED?

If you find yourself the recipient of an energy loss, or a psychic attack has left you debilitated (even after you did protection techniques), here are some things you can do to reset your energy:

Stomping. Simply hitting your heels hard on the ground, as if you were making the rhythmic sound of a drum, begins to knock out energies that are not helpful to you. Stomp to some kind of rhythmic music or drumming for at least 12 minutes, and it will help clear your energy field. Additionally, listening to the sound of a drum or drumming with the intention of clearing your energy field can work.

Hot shower / cold shower. Take a hot (or warm) shower, but then turn the knob to as cold as you can handle for a few minutes. If you can stand it, do a two-minute icy cold shower. It's highly beneficial. Then turn on the hot water again, to warm up, and end with another icy cold shower. You can repeat this several times. Rapidly going back and forth from hot to cold shakes off old energies. It's a bit like a dog who shakes hard to get water off his coat. The cold water is not just a shock to your physical body; it also shocks your energy field and, as a result, old energies can't cling on to you very easily. Additionally, scrubbing with salt, during either the hot phase or the cold phase will help restore your energy.

PROTECTING OTHERS

As a general rule, it is not appropriate use of energy to do protection methods on others without their permission. It also implies a kind of judgment about them—that they need protection. I wouldn't want someone to be placing a protective mantle around me without my permission . . . would you? Please don't do it.

However, this is completely different with your children. Surround them in a loving bubble of pink light in the morning as they trot off to school. Ask that angels embrace them in wings of light. Adopt a tree in their honor and ask that the tree protect them and keep them safe. You can also do protection methods with close family members, as your energies are already interwoven. One of my clients did a protection method for her husband, who was having severe breathing and coughing problems. He was also having a challenging time at work. His office environment had a lot of toxic energy. She didn't tell her husband that she was doing the protection process, but his coughing stopped at the exact time that she started, and his health catapulted into vitality. She said the results were remarkable.

Aiming Energy—Projecting Prayers

There are times when it might feel right to aim protective energy at another. Aiming energy is different from doing an energy protection; it is focusing an instant, potent stream of protective energy toward another. It is direct and deliberate . . . like a laser of light force. And it is used for emergencies. For example, if you see a dog crossing a busy road—and there's nothing you can physically do to protect him—instantly cast a shimmering, radiant ray to encapsulate him in protective light. You might imagine that this light cascades down from the heavens into your body, and then projects out of your solar plexus chakra or out of your heart chakra to him. Another example might be a child you see being mistreated in a store. You might intuitively sense that to chastise the parent might eventually cause more trauma for the child (who might be the recipient of the parent's anger at you for interfering). But you can aim energy and project prayers that surround the child and the parent with the energy of compassion, forgiveness, and love.

Additionally, if there is an area of the world in need, or in harm's way, you can pull out a map or bring up Google Earth on your computer, focus in on the area, and then proceed to aim energy and project protective prayers to that area. Hold the intention that it is for the highest good of all concerned.

In this chapter, you have learned about what energy protection is and have understood when it might not be a good idea. Additionally, you gained knowledge about psychic attacks, why they happen, and how to prevent and diminish them, as well as some awesome protection methods. In the next chapter, you will learn ways to stay in a balanced, strong energy field on a consistent basis.

CHAPTER FIVE

STRENGTHENING THE STRANDS THAT EMPOWER YOU

Everything in life is vibration.

— WIDELY ATTRIBUTED TO ALBERT EINSTEIN

Most people spend valuable time focusing on what they don't want and on what's not working in their life. They replay over and over something unfair that the boss said, or they wish their neighbor would move because they don't like the loud music they play, or they are unhappy because of their weight. However, it is an energy rule that what you focus on is what increases in your life. *Where intention goes, energy flows.* Someone who for years constantly thinks about how overweight they are often continues to be overweight. This can be because they will talk to everyone about how overweight they are, they will think about it incessantly, and they will judge themselves for it. They spend so much time focused on how overweight they are that it becomes their reality. Someone who is always ranting about the music of a neighbor often continues to have loud noises in their life.

In the previous chapters, you've learned what energy strands are and how to release ones that diminish you, as well as how to protect yourself. In this chapter, you will learn what you can do to increase the positive strands that connect you to the Universe, and how to keep your frequency humming along. You'll learn how to expand and plump up the strands that are anchored into you that are positive and glowing. This will bring you more vitality and will expand your life-force energy. You'll also learn how to create a sanctuary in your living space so that your personal energy field stays strong and vibrant.

COMMUNION CORDS WITH LOVED ONES . . . EVEN AT GREAT DISTANCES

I woke up in a panic.

"David, wake up!" I shook my husband to wake him up. He's a heavy sleeper, so it wasn't easy.

"What's happening?" he managed to groggily mumble, although he was still half asleep.

"I dreamed that Heather was in a small boat at night in high waves. It was really cold. One huge wave washed her overboard into an icy, dark sea. It was so real. I'm scared."

"Honey, go back to sleep. It was just a dream," he said as he rolled over and went back to a deep slumber.

But I couldn't go back to sleep. I loved my sister, Heather, and I was worried. Something was happening to her; I knew it. I immediately began projecting prayers toward her and surrounding her with protective white light.

At the time, Heather was working as a mariner on a research vessel, but I didn't know where in the world she was when I had the dream. After much tossing and turning and sending prayers, I finally fell asleep again. In the morning, I continued to surround her in a bubble of light.

Back in those days, there was no way to contact my sister when she was out at sea. So two weeks later, when she returned, I shared my dream with her. Heather was quiet for a long time, and then told me that on the exact night of my dream, she had been doing work on a ship off the Aleutian Islands in Alaskan waters. Eleven of the researchers and crew had gone ashore on a small island. But a storm emerged, and the waves became too rough to try to retrieve them and get them back to the ship.

The researchers and crew were going to be stranded on the beach on Unimak Island on a stormy, below-freezing night with no protective gear. The crew on the ship was extremely concerned about the survival of the people on the island. So Heather and another crewmember bravely decided to get into a small inflatable boat (called a Zodiac) and maneuvered through high waves to try to get the necessary survival suits to the island.

Huge wave after huge wave pounded over the Zodiac in the darkness. There were numerous points when Heather and the other crewmember were almost thrown overboard. She said it was a miracle that she survived. I like to think the energy I sent was helpful to her on that night.

This is an example of very special strands that I call "communion cords"; these are what hold families and loved ones together. Not only can we tune in to each other through them, but they also provide the comfort of knowing we are not alone. We know we have a clan of strength, love, and wisdom at our back. The clearer and more luminous the communion cords you have, the more balanced you will be.

When relationships are flourishing, these connecting strands are beautiful, glowing, thick, and strong. In people who have a long-term, loving commitment, or dearly care for each other, the strands glow, even though the individuals might have miles between them. Love, information, and emotions travel quickly and easily through communion cords. This is why a husband can tell his wife is in pain from slipping on the ice in front of the house even though he's at work. Or a mother can tell that her soldier son is in trouble even though he's far away at war. Or a twin can tell when her sibling is feeling elated even though they live in different towns. Communion cords connect us to our dear friends and family members, ancestors, beloved pets, and spiritual gurus, as well as to the angelic realms and the Creator. Life is harmonic and whole when our communion cords are clear and radiant.

However, sometimes in personal relationships, there is vibrational interference that creates debris within the communion strands that connect us. What this means is that although love flows through the cord connection, it isn't always as clear as it could be; there can be interference from people, places, and things. This phenomenon has been referred to as a kind of vibrational asteroid belt that pummels the strand. The vibrational interference that passes through the strands—like asteroids floating through a galaxy—makes the energy flow ragged and muddy. Hence, sometimes we'll misinterpret what is being said, or we'll feel that we are misunderstood. We feel that we have sent out a compassionate, kind communication, but when it reaches its destination, it is misunderstood and not taken the way we meant it.

This vibrational interference can come from other people, but it can also come from your location or your home energy. In this chapter, you'll learn a number of things you can do to keep your personal energy field strong and thus keep your communion strands vivid and effervescent. Here is an easy exercise that can clear out the detritus in the strands between you and a beloved.

21 DAYS TO SUMPTUOUS STRANDS

Step 1: Choose a specific time of day when you both have uninterrupted time available. Then choose the exact amount of time that you will be dedicating daily for 21 days. It can be anywhere from four to seven minutes; for example, every morning between 7:56 and 8:00 A.M.

Step 2: Make sure that your energy is as clear as possible. Shower or bathe beforehand. If that is not possible, then wash your face, hands, and feet.

Step 3: Sit facing in the direction of your beloved, no matter where he or she is. You might need to use a compass for this. (If you both are in the same physical location, sit across from each other.)

Step 4: Go into a meditative state and visualize the strands flowing between you as absolutely radiant, clear, and strong. They are so powerful that nothing can disrupt them.

This exercise is like going in for a tune-up for your car. It will make an enormous difference in your relationship. Down the road, if you feel that you need another tune-up, you can do it again. However, it usually doesn't need to be as long as 21 days. Even a few days can help reestablish the love strands between you both.

A HOME FOR THE SOUL

The energy in your home affects the energy of your life. The single most important influence on your strands is your home environment. If you want to have luscious, healthy, and clear affinity strands and communion strands, you need to live in a home that makes your heart sing. The energy of your home is the most valuable thing you can attend to in order to have bright energy connections to the greater world and to your loved ones. The energy in your home is an intersection between your inner universe and the outer universe, and between inner and outer realities. It can be a place of renewal and hope, a sanctuary within which you can retreat and recharge during changing times, an oasis of peace during turmoil. It can be a place of healing for every situation and a focal point for power and spirit. Not only can your home help to strengthen and heal you, but it can also be a template of harmony in which all who enter are invited to step up to a higher spiritual frequency. Everyone's energy strands will glisten with vibrant radiance as a result of the energy that you anchor into your home.

Your dwelling is much more than a place to lay your head and seek comfort from the elements. It's a crossing point in time and space that can attract energy or repel energy. And *every* object in your environment takes your energy up or down or keeps it neutral. These objects can uplift you or they can deplete you. Each object in your home affects your energy frequency, because you have strands and cords of energy connecting you to all the objects in your home.

It's valuable to infuse your living space with a sense of cosmic order to bring integrity and balance into your life. Your home can offer sanctuary and renewed faith during the times ahead; it can provide you with a sacred space within which you can remember who you are and why you're on the planet at this time. The energy of your home can either spur you toward gracious evolution or keep you stranded in one place.

Luckily, there are ways you can transform your home energy into a powerful force for good. By harmonizing your home and the things in it, and by releasing objects that do not reflect the life you desire now and in the future, you can open channels within your living space so that your home becomes a collection point for energy. Your home, in turn, will radiate this energy—in the form of love and light—to the rest of the world.

To establish your home as a sanctuary where you can renew your energy, replenish your inner resources, and strengthen your cords, there are several things you can do:

1. Clutter clear your home.

2. Space clear your home.

3. Create an altar in your home.

4. Establish remarkable vibrating energy fields in your home.

LESS CLUTTER, MORE JOY

Clutter clearing is one of the very best ways to keep your frequency high and your strands clear. You have strands of energy connecting you to each of the items in your home. The objects that have positive meaning for you, or that were given to you by someone with whom you have a loving relationship, will be clearer cords. If the relationship with the person who gave you an item is not a good one, usually the strands connecting you to that object are murky or limp. The associations and memories that an item has for you will also impact the strands attaching you to it. If there is a comforter on your bed that was your grandmother's, but your grandmother used to complain about life all the time, there might be an association with complaints about life connected to the comforter. This can affect your attached cords to the comforter and, as a result, how well you sleep.

Every item has a cord attaching to you at one of your chakras or energy centers. Your clutter subjects you to a mishmash of cords, strands, and filaments that are jamming up the works. This can make you feel exhausted, dragged down, and overwhelmed. When your energy strands are clogged, your life can feel clogged.

If you want to keep your strands vibrating with life force and strengthen the cords that connect you to the Universe, clear your clutter! Make your home energy shine!

One of the ways to release depleting strands is to clear out any "stuff" that you associate with a negative person, place, experience, or thing. If you feel that an ex-husband has strands hooked into you that you want to release but you have objects in your home that he gave you and that remind you of him, it might be time to do some clutter clearing. (Just because your ex gave you something doesn't mean that it necessarily is draining your energy, but often an object that has negative emotional associations will bring your energy down and can even strengthen the unhappy cords between you and the other person.)

After a divorce, separation, or breakup, one of the most important places to clutter clear is your bed. Sleeping in the same bed that the two of you shared often makes it difficult to detach from your ex. The cords between you can continue to reattach in spite of your cord cutting efforts. (Of course, if you can't afford a new mattress, then you can clear the old one with sage. Additionally, clear the headboard and frame. If you have a wooden bed frame, you can take a tuning fork and, after striking it, place the end on the wood so the vibration travels through the wood grain. If it is a metal bed, then use a bell or gong to clear it.)

From a spiritual perspective, letting go of physical stuff equates with letting go of emotional blockages and barriers in your life. In truth, clutter can be a signpost that indicates other things going on beneath the surface. It can also be a buffer in regard to various fears (such as the fear of rejection or fear about the future), or it might be the result of negative relationships, unresolved child-hood issues, feeling like you're not good enough, constantly nur-turing or pleasing others without taking care of your own needs, or a number of other things.

The cords and strands that connect us to our stuff can com-pletely clog our energy if we are not careful. The energy strands connecting us to the world around us can look like a rat's nest if our clutter is not addressed. Simply clearing the things that you don't love and don't use isn't enough. If you don't go to the *source* of the reason for the clutter, it will accumulate again and again.

More isn't better. Studies show that we are not happier, health-ier, smarter, or more loving as result of our stuff. We are in a super-sized society, and our homes are supersized with stuff. Clutter clearing as a physical activity is a valuable exercise; when you do it, there's less stuff to care for, clean, and trip over. However, in a deeper sense, clutter clearing can be a spiritually empowering exercise, because there comes a point when material objects begin to crowd out emotional and spiritual needs. Your cords become clogged with energetic debris.

Some people have a condition that propels them to hoard. This is very different from someone who just has an abundance of clutter. There is a very distinct brain pattern in hoarders that creates a need to hold on to objects; it is a physiological condi-tion, and this condition needs professional psychiatric support.

The information regarding clutter that I offer here doesn't apply to someone who has this unfortunate and debilitating condition.

In the end, it isn't about the stuff; it's about the meaning we invest in our stuff. For example, a pink vase might simply be a pink vase, but if it was the last thing that your love gave you before he went off to war—and he never returned—it might carry the meaning of true love. Or it might carry the meaning of guilt about his death (for example, if you encouraged him to go). Or it might carry the meaning of a love that can never be matched. It is not the object itself that creates challenges; it is the *meaning* that you invest in it. If you are having trouble having a positive romantic relationship and you have objects around you that represent failed relationships from the past, these objects subliminally continue to scream out to you, again and again, that you are a failure in regard to relationships. This in turn becomes a self-fulfilling prophecy.

In Chapter 2, you scanned your body to discover what you are corded to. You can use the same process to scan your home or living space to see what objects and items you have the strongest cords with. You can also scan to see if there is anything that brings your energy down and anything that you need to clear out of your home.

What is clutter to one person may not be to another. If you love it or use it, it is not clutter. Also, something that is clutter in one part of your home might not be clutter in another part. My suggestion is to go through your home, and with every object, ask yourself if you love it or use it. If the answer is no, you might consider moving it out of your living space. Your energy strands will thank you!

When you are in a clutter-free home, it's so much easier to release pesky strands and keep beneficial cords strong and clear. (For more information about clutter clearing, see my online certification program "Less Clutter, More Joy" to become a professional Clutter Coach through HayHouseU.com.)

The next step, after you have clutter cleared your home, is to clean it and then space clear it.

SPACE CLEARING TECHNIQUES

In ancient times, people understood the importance of creating a sense of harmony in their dwellings. They developed techniques and methods to release stagnant energy and to invoke joy and vitality in living spaces. Every ancient civilization and native culture used space clearing techniques. The methods and tools varied from one group to another, but the intent was the same—to create greater harmony and clarity in a living space. Native Americans used drums, rattles, and burning herbs in their rituals. The Chinese used gongs, chanting, and incense. In medieval Europe, salt and prayers cleared energy. In the Middle East, smoldering resins, such as frankincense and myrrh, were used to dispel negativity. Some of these traditions have survived virtually unchanged into modern times. The Greek Orthodox priest swinging an incense censer in a church and the person who throws salt over their shoulder to avert evil are both employing ancient techniques of space clearing, but many more have been lost to time.

For over four and a half decades, I have practiced the art of cleansing and harmonizing home energy, a skill that I named "space clearing." When I originated the phrase, I thought people would laugh, thinking it meant that someone had a broom up in space, but somehow the phrase stuck, and now it's in common usage. No matter what name is used, present-day space clearing techniques have their source in ancient techniques practiced throughout human history.

Clearing the Spaces in Your Home
Clears Space in Your Life

These ceremonies of old that brought vitality to human structures generations ago can be used to instill peace and equilibrium in today's homes and businesses. When your home is space cleared, it's very difficult for pesky strands of energy to stay anchored in your energy field. Many people are finding that these ancient rituals can be adapted very successfully for modern-day use, and most important, they are discovering that they work!

Following a century of rapid technological advances, people are recovering lost space clearing traditions. Traditional Western businesses are hiring professional space clearers because they have found that doing so increases sales and productivity. Some of the largest real estate firms in America are using the services of space clearers in order to dramatically accelerate property sales. Land management corporations are employing space clearers to perform blessings on the land before beginning to build large suburban housing developments. Homeowners who had never heard of space clearing only a year ago are now ringing bells, burning sage, and chanting mantras because they have found that their homes feel better as a result.

Your Home Energy Responds to Human Thought and Intention

Invisible yet very real strands of energy are interwoven throughout your home. Your home is not just an inanimate physical structure. It is a receptacle for vibrating, unseen energy fields ... and these energy fields respond to your thoughts and intention.

Every space has energy. Your home is not only a composite of materials assembled for shelter, but every cubic centimeter of it—whether solid or seemingly empty space—is also composed of infinite flows and strands of energy. When you enter a space that makes you immediately feel light and uplifted, or walk into a room where the atmosphere leaves you feeling depleted and drained, you are responding to the energy of the environment. If you notice tension and heaviness in a room after an argument has taken place, you are experiencing a residual energy that can linger in a space long after the argument has ended.

Sometimes energy in a home or office can become stagnant and dull. When this is the case, you may feel tired and listless or become agitated and angry. However, learning a few simple techniques to cleanse the energy of your space can produce a remarkable and positive influence on the way you feel and on every aspect of your life. When you call for blessings and assistance from the unseen realms of Spirit, negative strands drop away and untold magic and joy can fill your heart, so that your house becomes a home for your soul.

The most important requirements for any clearing will always be your own intuition and the promptings of your heart. As you open your heart to Spirit, you will be led to the tools, the information, and the ceremonies that are right for you.

Simply walking around each major room in your home ringing a bell, or lighting incense at an altar, or wafting the smoke of burning sage with a feather in the morning hours can set a template of clarity for the rest of the day. While you are space clearing your home, it's not uncommon for negative strands to drop off you as well. Here are a few steps to consider for your space clearing.

STEP-BY-STEP SPACE CLEARING

1. **Sit quietly.** Close your eyes and visualize that the space clearing brings crystal clear energy into your home. Your intuition is the key that will unlock the door into the revealing world of energy in your home.

2. **Drink plenty of water.** It is vital that you are hydrated before, during, and after the space clearing. The water will help transport energy through your body and will help release any unneeded energy that you may have taken on during the clearing.

3. **Put food away.** It is best not to leave open containers of food out during the clearing, as they may absorb energy.

4. **Remove jewelry.** Take off jewelry, particularly metal rings and bracelets. They can subtly impede your ability to sense energy during the space clearing. If that's not possible, don't be concerned; the clearing can still work.

5. **Focus your intention.** Be very clear on the results you desire for the home, the other occupants, and yourself.

6. **Sensitize your hands.** Breathe slowly and deeply. Sense the energy of the space. Circle the room or use any of your senses to perceive the energy in the room.

7. **Go slow.** Remember to silence your mind and go slowly with each step of the space clearing. This allows you to perceive subtle energy flows.

8. **Sense the energy in the space.** One of the skills necessary for space clearing is the ability to sense energy fields. To develop this skill, go around the periphery of a space very slowly with one hand extended. Notice areas where you feel a difference. Your arm may feel heavy or light, warm or cold in different places. There may be places that seem to feel sticky and places that feel smooth. This is not your imagination. You are sensing energy. (Usually the areas that feel sticky or heavy are the places that especially need clearing.) The secret to space clearing is to slow down, still your mind, and trust what you perceive.

9. **Stand at the entrance.** With equal weight on both feet, stand at the entrance of the room that you are going to clear. Take a few minutes to radiate your intention into the room and send prayers to the Creator for guidance and assistance.

10. **Break up the stagnant energy.** Take the tool that you are going to use (bell, gong, drum, burning herbs, essential oil mister) and, beginning at the entrance, walk in a circular manner with your tool with the intention that you are creating a wonderful vortex of energy. For example, if you are using a bell, ring the bell at just inside the entrance, and then walk in a circle around the room, ringing the bell, with the intention that the energy in that room will be sparkling!

11. **Smooth the energy of the space.** After you have cleared a room, smooth the energy of the space. To do this, you can run your hand gently around the periphery of the room, just as though you were petting a cat, until you sense that it feels settled and smooth. (You can also use a tool, such as a feather, to smooth the energy.)

12. **Invoke blessings.** After a room is cleared, imagine that it is filled with light and love while asking for support and guidance from the spiritual realms. You can pray silently or aloud to do this. This is the most important aspect of the clearing and must be done with reverence, respect, and devotion.

13. **Make a figure eight.** When you have completed a room, use your tool to make a figure eight to seal that room, then go to the next room. It's best to start at lower floors and then move upward in the house.

14. **Embrace gratitude.** At the completion, return to the front door, where you began, in a spirit of gratitude. When your home has been cleared in this way, it's difficult for negative energy strands to flow into your home. Additionally, it's difficult for you to have anything but positive strands flowing out of and into your body.

15. **Wash your hands.** Wash with cool water all the way to the elbows. Shake a few times before you dry your hands. The cold water and the shaking help release any energy that may have attached to your hands or body.

SPACE CLEARING TOOLS

Choosing a Space Clearing Tool

The tool that you use for space clearing is only a vehicle for your intention and prayers. By themselves, tools cannot sanctify a home. Your bell, drum, or gong only serves as a focus point for you to direct energy into a space. However, the tool that you choose is important, because when you feel a close connection to it, it serves to amplify your intention.

Choosing a tool for space clearing is very individual. One person may fall in love with the drum and find that every time they hear its sound, they can sense energy more perceptively. Someone else may find that burning sage creates a powerful shift of consciousness in a space. The best space clearing tool is the one that you feel most attracted to. How much you pay for it, or where it came from, does not matter as much as your love for it.

Empowering Your Space Clearing Tools

To empower your space clearing tool, hold it close to your body and visualize it becoming an extension of your body and soul. When you and your space clearing instrument are thus attuned to each other, there is a special kind of alchemy that strengthens every space clearing ceremony you perform.

Cleansing Your Space Clearing Tools

Before and after space clearing, you should cleanse the objects that you use. For example, if you use quartz crystals, place them in the sun or run clear, cold water over them to purify them. A drum, bell, or feather can be held in the smoke of smoldering sage leaves or cedar needles for cleansing. Your space clearing items should then be placed in a special place and kept clean. This is important, because it keeps a freshness and vitality around them.

Here are some of the tools that are traditionally used. These tools can be used for clearing your home and your cords and strands, and they can also be used for calling blessings and love into your home. The stronger and clearer the energy in your home, the stronger and more vibrant your strands will be.

Bells

There are beautiful bells made all around the world. Their sounds and the metals they are made from will vary with the traditions of their origin. Any bell can be used for space clearing if you feel a sense of connection with it and love its sound. The history and folklore surrounding bells could fill an entire book. Use your intuition to find the bell that is right for you.

Singing Bowls

The monk cradles the large metal bowl in his hand. His fingers rest gently on the cold, smooth surface as the weight of the bowl lies heavily on his palm. Focused and deliberate, he strikes the rim and slowly begins to circle the edge of the bowl with a wooden beater. A deep reverberating hum begins to build powerfully, majestically. His eyes close. His breathing becomes slow and deep. Sound fills him until he experiences disappearing into the sound. Ripples of sound undulate through him and fill the room. Softly laying down the mallet, he sits quietly until the sound becomes a whisper . . . then silence. Slowly opening his eyes, he looks at the space around him. The entire room seems to glisten with energy and light.

Tibetan singing bowls, sometimes called Himalayan bowls, come from Tibet, Nepal, or Northern India and have an outstanding ability to purify the energy in a home. Their use in Asia dates back to over 3,000 years ago. These remarkable objects can create a sound vibration so powerful it can feel as if the walls are coming down. The vibration of the sound seems to reach deep inside your soul. It can cleanse your strands and the myriad strands in your home. In fact, some Western doctors use singing bowls with cancer patients because they have found the sounds produced can have an impact on diseased cells.

When used for spiritual purposes, the sound of the singing bowl can also project powerful energy forms. Alexandra David-Néel, an intrepid French adventurer who spent 14 years exploring Tibet in the early 1900s, described seeing flashes of light coming out of a singing bowl played by a lama in a remote monastery. The holy man said the sound from the singing bowl could create shapes and even spiritual beings. He declared that one's thoughts and intentions could travel on the sound of the singing bowl to create manifestations of energy.

Crystal Singing Bowls

Quartz crystal singing bowls have a special ability to harmonize the subtle energy of light in a room as well as your personal energy field. They have a remarkable ability to clear any unneeded strands, especially any connecting into your third-eye and crown chakras. The energy produced by them is almost alchemical in nature and can dramatically raise the consciousness of a space. These bowls are made of silica, the base component of quartz crystals, and crystals have been used for spiritual practices for thousands of years. Quartz crystals have the ability to transmit information and energy and are used in the original quartz radios to transmit sound.

Crystal singing bowls range in size from 6 to 20 inches in diameter. Different sizes produce different tones. These ethereal-looking singing bowls can be played by gently tapping them with a padded wooden mallet to create a pure bell-like sound. You can also circle the circumference of the bowl with a rubber-coated mallet until it begins to sing. Be careful not to allow the vibration to become too intense for too long, as this can crack the crystal. The spiraling movement of the sound creates mystical spirals in the energy of the room.

Shamanic Drumming

Shamans have always used drums for banishing negative energy, clearing spaces, and releasing cords and attachments. Every earth-based culture throughout time has used drums for clearing negative energies and for inviting positive energy into a space.

Drumming is close to my soul, and I've seen profound results using the drum for clearing. I had drummed for decades, but when I was in Africa spending time with the Zulus, I had an experience that gave me an even deeper sense of the power of the drum. One night, I was sitting in the dirt in a hut made of straw and mud in Bophuthatswana, with the spiritual head of the Zulu Credo Mutwa. There was a fire in the center of his hut. Through the opening above the fire, I could see stars. It seemed that some of the small embers were floating up to join those sparkling pin-points of light. Next to Credo was a large, well-used drum that he was rhythmically tapping with his hands. The sonorous beat of his drum filled me—it felt like it was penetrating into the core of my being. Nothing existed except for the beat. Time had no beginning and no end. There wasn't dark and light, or good and bad . . . everything simply *was*. If it's true that the Universe is composed of a rhythmic, ever-changing, ever-flowing stream of energy, the drumbeat pushed me off the shore into the flow of that ancient and primordial sound, and I was being called home. This experience deepened my connection to my drumming.

For me, the drum provides a profound pathway to release entity attachments, dissolve dark energies, clear energy fields of negative strands, and invite excellent, loving energy into a room or space. I've used the drums many times to clear dark energies.

I'm a drum-maker, so I have a special connection to drums. My husband and I have been making drums for decades. We also drum together. We drum to connect with the cycles of life, to celebrate our lives, to release pent-up emotions, and to grow closer to the Creator. I also teach drumming and lead drumming circles. The drum is one of my allies. It carries me to the center of my soul. And one of its gifts is the ability to clear spaces and people.

The sound of drumming is part of our genetic code. The sound tunes us in to ancestral memories of our collective tribal life around the fire. Its rhythmic beat is the pulse, the heartbeat, of the Universe. As with singing in some Native American tribes, drumming is believed to open a mystical pathway so drummers can connect with our Creator, the Great Mystery. In the shamanic traditions of Siberia, it's believed that drumming creates a bridge so you can go from one world to another. When you stop playing the drum, the bridge disappears.

DRUMMING TO SPACE CLEAR

1. **Greet your drum**. By slowly rubbing your hand around in a circle on your drum, you are greeting it. Address it by name or with a reverent title, such as Star Singer or Mother's Heartbeat.

2. **Hold your drum close to your heart**. Imagine love flowing into it. Allow your awareness to fill the interior of the drum.

3. **Be still and allow the energy inside you to build**. When the energy is at its peak, express it as a shout or just begin to drum. This calls Spirit and asks for assistance.

4. **Begin drumming**. Keep your drumstick hand really loose. Allow your wrist to be flexible so the movement comes from the wrist instead of the arm. The heartbeat two-beat rhythm—*lub-dub*—is good to start out. It's a primal sound for humans. We all heard this rhythm in the womb.

5. **Allow your breath to deepen and your body to relax**. Let the rhythm emerge of its own accord. Use whatever beat feels best to you, simply allowing a natural rhythm to evolve. Trust your intuition. Get out of the way and allow the drumming to happen. Connect with the spirit of the drum.

6. **Drum until the entire room rings clear.** Your intuition will tell you when this is complete.

7. **Make a figure eight with your drum.** In other words, hold your drum in front of you and move it as if you were creating a figure eight in front of you. This seals the circle of energy. When the figure eight is complete, you should be in the same corner or area where you started.

8. **Thank the Creator for assisting you.** Express gratitude audibly or silently. Then be still and allow Spirit to fill the space and you.

Objects that are used for space clearing are used much in the same way that they are used for cord cutting. The difference between drums and other space clearing tools is that drums can break up heavy, dense, thick energy quickly. Bells, chimes, essential oils, feathers, and incense, on the other hand, are better suited for more subtle energy.

Rattles: Calling Spirit

Not all tribes used drums, but the use of ceremonial rattles is nearly ubiquitous. I love working with rattles. For me personally, it's often easier to call Spirit with a rattle than with a drum. Somehow the softer sound seems to lull me into an expanded awareness of the world around me. In the present day, rattles are used to soothe babies. This custom has its roots in native cultures where rattles were used to ward off negative spirits, so using a rattle with a child was thought to keep the child safe and protected.

Rattles were also used to clear negative energies and create an energy of protection and grace. Native rattles were made from a variety of materials, such as gourds, turtle shells, pottery, rawhide, and even carved wood, and they were decorated in a symbolic manner, with every part of the décor having a deeper meaning.

Just as drums were considered sacred because their rhythm created a bridge from the physical world to the spiritual world, the cadence of native rattles also has the ability to alter consciousness and transport us to other realms.

Whenever you shake a rattle, you'll activate genetic memories of dancing around a fire, and its sound can softly clear cords of energy that don't serve you or your home, as well as flooding beneficial energy into your environment. Simply taking a rattle and running it down your body while you rattle—starting at your head and working downward—you can space clear your energy field and the energies around you, as well as clear most minor attachments and unneeded strands, *and* increase the energy of your positive strands.

STRENGTHEN YOUR STRANDS TO THE UNIVERSE

One of the most effective ways to bring a balanced, vibrant energy into your home is through the use of a home altar. Home altars go back to the earliest history of human beings, even into primordial times, when people lived in caves. Altars made out of bear bones and other objects have been found on cave ledges. Now, in modern times, we have echoes of this practice. For example, a gathering of photos on the home piano is a kind of subliminal ancestor altar. The objects that you gather above your fireplace echo back to altars honoring Hestia in ancient Greece, in which altars by the fireplace blessed home and hearth.

Altars do not need to be religious; simply gathering together objects that are meaningful to you can energize your home. Altars are valuable because they provide a spiritual backdrop for everything that occurs in your home. They also serve as a kind of beacon to call spiritual assistance and then radiate sparkling energy into the space.

Why Altars Work

In many ways, the power of the altar lies in its visible appearance. The structure and objects of the altar appeal to our psyche because they give form to the formless and provide a visual representation of the Divine. It is difficult to comprehend the spiritual realm because of its unseen nature. However, when objects are thoughtfully placed on an altar to physically represent thoughts, plans, ideas, or dreams—which by their very essence are invisible—this gives substance to your intentions.

The creation of an altar is a sacred act, an act of power and grace. For a few timeless minutes, as you stand before your altar, you enter a dimension beyond ordinary reality, where light, sound, and energy merge into an exquisite state of being. The creation of an altar to strengthen your strands to the Universe is a hallowed thing. It sets forces in play that will continue to radiate light and a vibrant frequency through all of your strands, and this can have a profound effect on all of the cords, ribbons, strands, and filaments of energy that flow out of you, into you, and in and out of your home.

Create Your Altar from Scratch

1. A place for your altar. There are many methods you may use to determine a place for your altar; however, the best place is the place that works for you. No space is too small to make an effective and lovely altar. Size is not important. What matters is combining your clear intention with your very best efforts to create a lovely spot representative of what is in your heart. It can be on a shelf, a hearth, a window ledge, a coffee table, a dresser, or the floor.

2. Preparation for your altar. After you have decided where to put your altar, gather your materials together. Select the objects that will be included in the altar, decide how you will arrange them on the altar, and finally, cleanse the energy of both objects and space. Decide what overall feeling you wish to portray. Take your time with this step—you are setting the stage and the energy for everything that will come after.

This preparation is a very important step in the creation of your altar because the basic energy of your altar is established during its inception. The ongoing energy of your altar is dependent upon the care and thoroughness that you put into these preparation stages.

3. Your altar cloth. The altar cloth can provide a kind of context—a grounding—for the rest of the altar. It represents the foundation that the altar is built upon. Altar cloths can add a richness and depth of dimension to any altar. Choose colors and textures that give you the feeling you desire for your affinity strands. Here are some common associations with the different colors you might choose for your altar cloth:

- **Red:** Activity, courage, physical strength, grounding
- **Orange:** Optimism, social connection, enthusiasm, endurance
- **Yellow:** Mental clarity, happiness, cheerfulness
- **Green:** Growth, abundance, healing, harmony, hope
- **Blue:** Faith, trust, communication, sincerity, wisdom
- **Purple:** Nobility, grace, spiritual attunement, dignity
- **Violet:** Connection to spiritual and angelic realms
- **Pink:** Love, sincerity, innocence
- **White:** Light, purity, simplicity, cleanliness
- **Black:** Strength, power, elegance, depth, wisdom

4. Representation of the Divine. Every altar should have an object on it that represents spiritual or divine energies. At least one altar item should symbolically represent a dimension beyond the ordinariness of life. For one person, this might be something from nature; for someone else, it might be a picture of a spiritual teacher or an ancient god; for another, an icon of Jesus or Mary or the Buddha. Having an altar object that signifies a realm beyond the physical realms declares your altar to be a sacred space.

5. Representation of you (and friends and family members). It's important that you are represented on your altar, so put something on it that signifies you. It can be a photograph, but you can also use a crystal, stone, or memento. You can also include objects that represent other people, to make sure that you have beneficial strands flowing between you. On my altar, I put a small, hand-carved stone mother bear to represent me, a father bear for my husband, and a baby bear for our daughter. I positioned them so we were all facing each other, and I put a rose-quartz heart in the center of our small circle.

6. Dedication of your altar. A dedication ceremony invokes energy into the altar, to activate it and bring positive, beneficial energy to you and your family and friends. Here is an example of a dedication:

"May the Creator who dwells within all things bring blessings to this home. May this altar be a constant reminder of the Divine spark of joy that dwells in each of us. Let joy, love, guidance, and peace fill these items and the altar upon which they reside. May these items bless our home with inner peace and joy."

7. Preservation of the energy of your altar. Once the energy of your altar has been established, you will want to keep it fresh and renewed so that it can always be a source of strength and peace for you. There are a number of ways you can do this. The simplest way—and one of the most powerful—is to regularly meditate at your altar. Meditating at your altar clears the items on it, and the strands that connect you to your inner and outer worlds are strengthened.

The power of your prayers and intention infuses the altar with energy, which radiates out into the Universe, magnifying what is in your heart, so that it becomes a force for healing and action in the world. This energy rebounds back to you as well, so that you feel filled with more life and peace. This is a two-way process that can have an incredible effect on your life, even as it works to continually add to the potency of your altar.

Stones and Gemstones on Your Altar and in Your Home

Polished stones and gemstones have been used on altars (and in personal living spaces) and for healing purposes since the earliest times. It was felt that each type of stone or gem could elicit a particular and unique kind of energy. Some activated healing and were used for soothing and relaxing, while others were used to evoke vitality. Using specially chosen stones or gems on your home altar can quicken the specific kind of energy associated with them. Here are some qualities commonly associated with some gems and stones:

- **Agate**: Success, happiness
- **Amber**: Protection, healing
- **Amethyst**: Compassion, clairvoyance
- **Aquamarine**: Harmony
- **Aventurine**: Healing
- **Bloodstone**: Healing, physical strengthening
- **Carnelian**: Physical grounding
- **Citrine**: Mental clarity
- **Emerald**: Spiritual healing
- **Fluorite**: Mental attunement, calming
- **Garnet**: Physical strength, assertiveness
- **Jade**: Healing, wisdom
- **Jet**: Grounding, protection
- **Lapis lazuli**: Spirituality, intuition, royalty
- **Malachite**: Psychic power, healing, cleansing
- **Moonstone**: Emotional balancing, lunar qualities

- **Obsidian**: Grounding, protection
- **Opal**: Emotional clarity
- **Peridot**: Mental and physical healing, rejuvenation
- **Prehnite**: Calmness, unconditional love, healing
- **Quartz crystals**: Spiritual attunement
- **Ruby**: Strength, health, and spiritual passion
- **Sapphire**: Devotion and spirituality
- **Selenite**: Dreaming skills, intuition, meditation
- **Topaz**: Expansion, knowledge
- **Tourmaline**: Purification, healing, protection
- **Turquoise**: Healing, balancing

Stones that you gather from nature can also be sources of healing energy. Similarly, a stone given to you by someone special will contain the energy of that connection. Placing these stones on your altar is one way of implanting that energy in the space.

Plant and Flower Offerings

On altars throughout the world, you will find offerings of fruit, flowers, and grains. These are traditionally used because they represent the bounty brought forth from the Earth Mother. A glowing orange, a small bowl of rice, a beautiful arrangement of bright flowers—all of these things add richness, beauty, and a feeling of abundance to the altar, as well as anywhere else they are placed in the home. They call in these qualities, and can secure them in the energy of the home.

CALLING ANGELS INTO YOUR HOME

One of the most profound things you can do to invite blessings into your home is to invoke the angelic energies. Here is a very simple method to do this to fill your home with remarkable light and sparkling vitality: Simply light a candle, quiet your mind, and hold the intention that the angels remove all strands that are not needed from you, from other occupants in your home, and from your home itself. Imagine a large angel behind you, enveloping you in his or her wings of light. Let go, surrender, and trust that all is well.

There is a secret that allows this method to be the most powerful of all methods. For it to work, it's valuable to believe in angels and trust that they can sever all that is not needed. Angels are real . . . even if you don't believe in them. However, if you do believe in them, this method is much more effective.

I've had some experiences that I'd love to share with you about angels in hopes of deepening your connection to the angelic realm. I didn't believe in angels before I had angelic experiences. Now I know that angels are just a thought away—and simply reading about angels here begins to create even more loving strands between you and the angelic realms.

My first vivid experience of angels was when I was in the hospital as a 17-year-old, as a result of my very traumatic injuries. One night, I woke up in extreme pain. I squeezed my eyes shut; the slightest exertion seemed to tear me open. I couldn't get away from it; the pain rolled over me, wave after wave. I silently pleaded for someone to help me.

I heard the door creak open, followed by the sound of footsteps. Then I felt a hand gently slip into mine. Immediately, the pain subsided, and a wonderful feeling of safety flooded my being. I opened my eyes, expecting to see the nurse or doctor who had kindly come in to comfort me, but the room was empty!

And yet I could still feel the warmth and texture of a hand squeezing mine. *Someone's* hand was in my hand. I couldn't see anyone, but I could feel their fingers and their fingernails. It was undeniable. A feeling of peace and relaxation slowly washed over me, and I fell into a deep sleep. After that night, whenever I was in pain, comforting hands came to soothe me in the night hours. Sometimes the hand felt male, sometimes female. At one point, I remember a very small, childlike hand holding mine. I was so grateful for the presence of what I now know are angels.

Since that time many years ago, angels have come into my life in many forms. Most of the time, they come as a sudden insight or intuition. Sometimes they come invisibly, as they did when I was in the hospital. But sometimes, under rare circumstances, they come in a physical form, looking human but with a heavenly presence.

I was 18 years old. After I got out of the hospital, life was hard. I was living at a trailer court by the side of the freeway, washing dishes at a truck stop to try to earn money to go to college. I didn't know anyone, and I felt so lonely. The winter nights were especially hard for me. The cold wind and constant noise of the freeway seeped in through the metal seams of my trailer. The harshness of my job and the despair about my life seemed overwhelming at times, and I'd often fall asleep sad and exhausted.

One chilling winter night, at about 3 A.M., I woke up gravely despondent. I'd had enough. I wanted out of my life. A dead calm came over me. I knew what I had to do.

With grim determination, I walked out of my trailer, down the road, and eventually across a large park on my way to the bridge. The ground was covered with patches of dirty snow. As I walked through the park, which was lit by street lamps, I saw a young man about my age sitting on a park bench with his head hung low. Normally, I would have never approached a total stranger at 3 A.M. in such an isolated area. But since I was going to end it all that night anyway, I thought, *What does it matter if he tries to hurt me? I'm going to be dead in a few moments anyway. I have nothing to lose.*

I walked up and asked if he was okay. He looked up at me and shook his head and murmured, "No, I'm not."

I sat down next to him. He proceeded to tell me about some troubles in his life, and eventually confided that he was on the way to the bridge to kill himself too.

We chatted for a long time. I said, "Hey, you're young. You're going through a rough time, but things will get better."

He perked up, told me how much I'd helped him, and thanked me profusely. I felt so good that I forgot about drowning myself, and I turned around and went back home. As I walked back through the park, the sun was rising. The patches of snow that had previously looked dingy and sullied now glowed pink and looked beautiful against the dark earth. As I stepped into my trailer, I knew that, although I was going through a rough period, things would get better . . . and they did.

Years later, I realized that my encounter wasn't by chance. I believe that on that frigid winter night, I met an angel . . . a real angel. Of course, there's no way to know for sure, but that man will always be an angel to me.

Angels come in many forms; however, most often they're unseen. Not only have I been blessed in my life with invisible angelic visitations, but numerous people in my seminars have also experienced the same thing.

I was teaching a course about angels in Ireland when something remarkable occurred. In one exercise, I asked people to raise their right arm into the air. A man in the center of the room was in a wheelchair because he had a very serious debilitating disease. He was dismayed that, because of his illness, he was unable to lift his arms, and he really wanted to follow the instructions. Suddenly, he felt someone from behind lift his arm. When he turned to see who it was, no one was there.

Nevertheless, he could still feel the fingers and hand of someone holding his arm up, *and there was an indentation in his arm where it was being held.* Five times, I asked participants to raise their arm, and five times, the invisible hand lifted his arm. His wife, who sat next to him, also saw the indentations in his upper arm, as if an unseen hand held his arm high. At the completion of the course, the couple came to me, their eyes glistening with tears. They felt that they'd witnessed a miracle.

Although angels are usually unseen, they can also appear in human form, like the angel who appeared when I was having coffee with my friend Andrea in London. At the time, she was the editor in chief of one of the world's largest magazines. We were sitting in a tiny, deserted café, huddled around our small table, chatting about the events in our lives. We were concluding our conversation, when a striking woman who looked to be in her 70s, with white coiffed hair and a pink suit, came into the café.

She ordered a cappuccino, walked directly to our table, and asked if she could join us.

Andrea and I were both startled by her request. All the other tables were empty, and ours barely had room for us. Yet we agreed that she could join us. She sat down, placed her coffee in front of her, turned to Andrea, and began to speak as if the words flowed straight from her soul into the heart of my friend.

The insight and guidance she offered about Andrea's life was remarkable. At one point, Andrea and I looked at each other as if to say, *Isn't this incredible!* and when we looked back, the woman was gone . . . completely gone! She wasn't in the café, and she wasn't down the street. She had literally vanished. We stared in amazement at her full cappuccino and then back at each other. Andrea leaned forward and whispered, "That was an angel!"

I nodded in agreement. "That *was* an angel."

Angels are real . . . and they are here to help us. They are simply a thought away. Call upon them. Ask for their support as you clear away strands and energy cobwebs that do not empower you or support you, in your personal energy field and in the energy field of your home.

Conclusion

Thank you for sharing this journey with me into the nature of energy strands. As I mentioned in the Preface, my beloved Hawaiian teacher told me, "When you understand the nature of these strands, you stand at the center of all that is real and important in life. You know how to stand in the center of grace and personal power." Her words have guided me through the decades. They initiated my journey of understanding that we are not separate from the Universe around us—that we are a part of a vast, pulsating ocean of energy that is constantly interacting with us.

We are not only influenced by the consciousness of this sea of life force, but we are each an integral, essential, living part of it. We are infinitely interconnected with it all. Great flotillas of energy strands surge out from each of us into a realm where time and space are illusions, where the past, present, and future all exist in a continuous here now.

The journey to follow our individual and collective strands to the farthest shore of the vast Universe is a hallowed and sacred one. I'm honored to have been with you on this path, my fellow soul travelers, as we have explored the filaments, threads, ribbons, strands, and cords of energy that tie us to everything in the world. Together, we've learned how to tell what we are most strongly connected to and what takes our energy up and as well as down, in addition to numerous ways to sever the cords that bind us and increase and magnify the strands that empower us.

I hope that I have been a gentle companion along the way as you have read this book. And it is my sincere wish that the information you gained in these pages is valuable to you on your travels through life.

Acknowledgments

A big thank-you to my gracious editor, Sally Mason-Swaab, and to the excellent copy editor Rachel Shields. And an immense thank you to Meadow Linn, my lovely daughter, and David Linn, my stalwart husband, for reminding me what's truly important in life. And a huge depth of gratitude to the remarkable Patti Allen, Terry Bowen, Kelly Chaumchuk, LuAnn Cibik, Laura Clark, and Felicia Messina D'Haiti . . . you guys kept the home fires burning while I was writing this book. My gratitude goes beyond words.

About the Author

Denise Linn's personal journey began as a result of a near-death experience at age 17. Her life-changing experiences and remarkable recovery set her on a spiritual quest that led her to explore the healing traditions of many cultures, including those of her own Cherokee ancestors, the Aborigines in the Australian bush, and the Zulus in Bophuthatswana. She trained with a Hawaiian kahuna (shaman), and Reiki Master Hawayo Takata. She was also honorarily adopted into a New Zealand Maori tribe. In addition, Denise lived in a Zen Buddhist monastery for more than two years.

Denise is an internationally renowned teacher in the field of self-development. She's the author of the bestseller *Sacred Space* and the award-winning *Feng Shui for the Soul,* and has written 19 books, which are available in 29 languages, and hosts a popular weekly radio show. Denise has appeared in numerous documentaries and television shows worldwide and gives seminars throughout the world.

Denise lives in Northern California on a mountain amidst the pines with her husband, David. Their daughter, Meadow, is the co-author of *The Mystic Cookbook.* For information about Denise's workshops and lectures, please visit her website: www.DeniseLinn.com.

Hay House Titles of Related Interest

YOU CAN HEAL YOUR LIFE, the movie,
starring Louise Hay & Friends
(available as an online streaming video)
www.hayhouse.com/louise-movie

THE SHIFT, the movie,
starring Dr. Wayne W. Dyer
(available as an online streaming video)
www.hayhouse.com/the-shift-movie

———

CHAKRAS: Seven Keys to Awakening and Healing the Energy Body,
by Anodea Judith

ONE MIND: How Our Individual Mind Is Part of a Greater Consciousness and Why It Matters, by Larry Dossey, M.D.

THE POWER OF LOVE: Connecting to the Oneness, by James Van Praagh

SOUL JOURNEYING: Shamanic Tools for Finding Your Destiny and Recovering Your Spirit, by Alberto Villoldo

All of the above are available at your local bookstore,
or may be ordered by contacting Hay House (see next page).

———

We hope you enjoyed this Hay House book. If you'd like to receive our online catalog featuring additional information on Hay House books and products, or if you'd like to find out more about the Hay Foundation, please contact:

Hay House, Inc., P.O. Box 5100, Carlsbad, CA 92018-5100
(760) 431-7695 or (800) 654-5126
(760) 431-6948 (fax) or (800) 650-5115 (fax)
www.hayhouse.com® • www.hayfoundation.org

———

Published in Australia by: Hay House Australia Pty. Ltd.,
18/36 Ralph St., Alexandria NSW 2015
Phone: 612-9669-4299 • *Fax:* 612-9669-4144
www.hayhouse.com.au

Published in the United Kingdom by: Hay House UK, Ltd.,
The Sixth Floor, Watson House, 54 Baker Street, London W1U 7BU
Phone: +44 (0)20 3927 7290 • *Fax:* +44 (0)20 3927 7291
www.hayhouse.co.uk

Published in India by: Hay House Publishers India,
Muskaan Complex, Plot No. 3, B-2, Vasant Kunj, New Delhi 110 070
Phone: 91-11-4176-1620 • *Fax:* 91-11-4176-1630
www.hayhouse.co.in

———

Access New Knowledge.
Anytime. Anywhere.

Learn and evolve at your own pace
with the world's leading experts.

www.hayhouseU.com